What peop

The End of the Beginning

Julia's story is raw, honest and beautiful. She has written more than an autobiography or a memoir; she has written a pilgrimage. Her words reveal her courage, brokenness and pain, but they also reveal a God who is gracious, compassionate and restorative. I was deeply moved as I read of her remarkable journey, and felt like I was walking on holy ground. This book is inspiring, but it is also challenging. It invites us to make our own holy expeditions into the land of hope and grace.

Malcolm Duncan (FRSA)
Pastor, author, theologian, broadcaster

A deeply personal, yet powerfully encouraging, book on how to navigate tragedy well. In *The End of the Beginning*, Julia Lawton shares her story of being widowed with three small children. While she does not sidestep the deep pain of loss, the reader is continually brought back to the goodness, grace and power of a loving God to bring hope and healing out of heartache. Whatever grief you might be facing, allow Julia's story to take your hand and gently walk the journey with you out of darkness and into the light of a new tomorrow.

Jen Baker
Author and speaker

Julia's excellent book is the perfect companion for anyone who has experienced loss of any kind. We all go through tough valleys and need the wisdom, kindness and brutal honesty of somebody who has been there and lived to tell the tale. I can't recommend this hope-filled book enough. It moved and inspired me in equal measure.

Cathy Madavan
Writer, speaker and broadcaster

This is a wonderful book! In sharing her story, Julia brings genuine insight, encouragement and practical help for all who have experienced grief and loss. With honesty and tenderness, her journey is about more than simply surviving; it is about finding new life in Jesus Christ and the new hope and purpose He brings.

Chris Cartwright
General superintendent, Elim Pentecostal Churches

Julia has not had an easy life. She has faced a long journey of grief since her husband died a sudden death in 1986 and left her a young widow with three small children. In this book, which tells her story, she is honest about the cycle of grief. Her journey teaches us that grief is not linear or a process we move through. It leaves scars.

After meeting Simon, her second husband, and coping with their growing family, she has had to learn that these scars leave an impression. But Julia serves a loving God who draws close to the brokenhearted. During Nigel's illness, Julia learned that God was interested in her. Throughout her Christian life she has had to allow God to anoint the scars and allow her to heal.

This is an honest and real account of a journey through grief and how it can cast a dark shadow over life. But God shines through more brightly.

Debbie Duncan
Author and speaker

This excellent book is essential reading for anyone dealing with loss or bereavement. Written with honesty, transparency and vulnerability, readers may find themselves deeply moved, while at other times laughing out loud because of the warmth and humour of its style. We unreservedly recommend it.

John and Marilyn Glass
Former General Superintendent, Elim Churches and former Chair of Council Evangelical Alliance
Former National Leader of Aspire, Elim Churches national women's ministry

Julia's courage and honesty shine through in this book about her journey through grief with Jesus. She tells her story with vulnerability and humility, allowing God's goodness to take centre stage in every chapter. Julia's story is testament to a God who is patient, kind and faithful, and who does more than we could ever ask or imagine. It's an encouragement that there is always hope, even in the darkest of times.

Bekah Legg
CEO Restored

From the outset, Julia opens her heart and invites the reader into a moment in time when tragedy hit her world. She doesn't gloss over the devastating events that occurred back then, but chooses to be real, honest and vulnerable. Julia writes with understanding and insight about the various stages of grief she encountered as a young widow and mother. Her conversational approach is comforting; brimming with empathy and compassion. I believe Julia's journey through grief will not only inspire and bring relief to the bereaved, but will also help to equip those who know someone who has. This book truly is a story of hope in the midst of grief and loss.

Lara Martin
Funeral celebrant, pastor and music minister

Julia's story gives an honest account of the grief, pain and emotion she experienced after losing her husband. Her story gives hope to anyone who has suffered a loss, as it's a testimony of how God restores, rebuilds and heals a broken heart. Throughout this book, Julia not only shares her journey with grief, but also gives scriptures and advice that will help many others who can relate to her experience. Julia's desire is that you will also be able to walk in freedom as you allow God to minister to you in your grief.

Leanne Mallett
National Leader of Aspire, Elim's Churches national women's ministry

This is such an inspiring read! Julia's story, which she shares with such honesty and vulnerability, leads us on a journey towards hope and freedom. *The End of the Beginning* is a reminder to us all that it's not the end; it's just a bend. Dive into this book and be encouraged.

Amy Summerfield CEO, Kyria Network and head of development, Skylark International, Zeo Church

The End of the Beginning

A story of hope in the midst of grief and loss

Julia Lawton

ISBN 978-1-9996489-4-7
e-ISBN 978-1-9996489-5-4
First edition 2021

Acknowledgements
Scripture quotations are primarily taken from the Holy Bible, New International Version Anglicised. Copyright © 1979, 1984, 2011 Biblica, formerly International Bible Society. Used by permission of Hodder & Stoughton Ltd, an Hachette UK company. All rights reserved. "NIV" is a registered trademark of Biblica. UK trademark number 1448790.

Scripture quotations marked (MSG) are taken from The Message. Copyright © 1993, 1994, 1995, 1996, 2000, 2001, 2002. Used by permission of NavPress Publishing Group.

Scripture quotations marked (NKJV) are taken from the New King James Version®. Copyright © 1982 by Thomas Nelson. Used by permission. All rights reserved.

Scripture quotations marked (NLT) are taken from the Holy Bible, New Living Translation, copyright © 1996, 2004, 2007, 2013, 2015 by Tyndale House Foundation. Used by permission of Tyndale House Publishers, Inc., Carol Stream, Illinois 60188. All rights reserved.

Scripture quotations marked (NASB) are taken from the New American Standard Bible®, Copyright © 1960,1962,1963,1968,1971,1972,1973,1975,1977,1995 by The Lockman Foundation. Used by permission.

Scripture quotations marked (AMP) are taken from the Amplified® Bible. Copyright © 2015 by The Lockman Foundation. Used by permission.

Scripture quotations marked (AMPC) are taken from the Amplified® Bible, Classic Edition. Copyright © 2015 by The Lockman Foundation. Used by permission.

Scripture quotations marked (ESV) are taken from the ESV® Bible (The Holy Bible, English Standard Version®). ESV® Text Edition: 2016. Copyright © 2001 by Crossway, a publishing ministry of Good News Publishers. The ESV® text has been reproduced in cooperation with and by permission of Good News Publishers. All rights reserved.

A catalogue record for this book is available from the British Library.

I would like to dedicate this book to Nigel and Simon.
To have one great marriage is amazing, but to have two is even more
amazing... and for that I am incredibly grateful to God.

Acknowledgements

I am so grateful to those who have been involved in my journey. I could name many, but the list would go on and on, so I'll focus on my family.

Thanks to my late parents Dick (Richard Henry) and Betty (Florence Elizabeth) Woodford, who gave me a very privileged and loving upbringing. They taught me good morals, which have stood me in good stead as I have navigated my way through life.

To the Toone family: Nigel's dad Roland and his sisters Ann, Elaine and Chris, along with their husbands, Dave, Sam and Steve, for always being there for me, especially just after Nigel died when they were struggling with their own grief. They may not always have agreed with my choices, but they never let me down.

To my sisters, Jackie, Katrina and Suzanne, who have given their love, support and encouragement in numerous ways over the years.

To the Lawtons, who welcomed me into their family from the first time I met them, and especially to Janet and Phil, who regularly babysat and took the boys on all kinds of adventures.

To my sons, Matthew, Stuart and Ashley for being such good little boys. This made looking after them easy after their dad died, and they have grown up into such lovely men, making me a very proud mum.

To my daughters, Sarah and Amy, who made our family complete and who have grown up into such kind, caring young women. They have encouraged me every step of the way in writing this book and also make me very proud.

Finally, a massive thank you to Simon for marrying a young widow and becoming an instant father to three little boys. He has supported, encouraged and always been there for me, and put up with me when I didn't make his life easy. He loved me when I was unlovable and has helped me become the woman God has called me to be. When I felt I couldn't finish writing this book, he cajoled and encouraged me to finish, and when I felt overwhelmed after the first edit he spent hours helping me do the work that was needed on it. Without his love and support my journey would have been a lot tougher. I love him more now than ever.

I count myself really blessed that I had so many people around me to comfort, support and care for me at a time of inexpressible grief and loss. Thank you to every single one of you from the bottom of my heart.

Contents

Introduction

Writing this book was probably the hardest thing I have ever had to do. I've had to dig deep into my past to places that have caused me a lot of anguish, hurt and pain, and it has bought things to the surface that I believed I had already dealt with.

My husband Simon has been saying for many years that I should sit down and write my story, and on various occasions people have spoken over my life that there is a book in me. I have always shied away from this, as it's not something I thought I would ever be able to do. Perhaps you will begin to understand why as you read my story.

In 2020, when Covid-19 hit and all that seemed familiar changed across the globe, I found myself out of work, so this felt like the right moment to actually sit down and share my story with you. I made a start but felt I couldn't continue; however, a young friend of mine, Ratidzo Parirenyatwa, regularly texted or called to ask me how it was going. I told her I couldn't continue with it, but she persisted. So one day I thought to myself, "I may never get the opportunity to have so much spare time again. Okay, let's do it!"

My heart's desire is that something of what I share will help you navigate the life set before you. For those of you who have been bereaved, my heart goes out to you. You may never fully get over losing that loved one, but you will learn to live with the loss and move forward into the future God has planned for you.

I will never forget or stop loving my first husband, Nigel. I only have to look at my three wonderful sons to be reminded of him. However, I thank God that his death wasn't the end for me, but rather a new beginning. This new season in my life is all the better because of the life I had experienced beforehand. I know now that I can't take life for granted. We must live our lives one day at a time, without bearing grudges and always forgiving people, even when we feel something wasn't our fault. Life is too short, as I discovered. We must learn to embrace every day as if it is our last, and to make the most of every opportunity.

> *"Show me, Lord, my life's end and the number of my days; let me know how fleeting my life is. You have made my days a mere handbreadth; the span of my years is as nothing before you. Everyone is but a breath, even those who seem secure"* (Psalm 39:4-5).

My desire for this book is to share my story so that others who are grieving the loss of a loved one will realise they are not alone, that what they are experiencing is normal and that there is real hope in Jesus Christ.

Nigel Toone (14th February 1953 to 3rd July 1986)

The following funeral tribute, written by fellow cricketer Dr David Wilson, appeared in a charity match programme played between Rothley Imps Football Club and Rothley Park Cricket Club on 12th October 1986 to raise funds for Nigel's family.

Nigel Toone's untimely death in early July, at the age of thirty-two, left Rothley stunned. Words can hardly begin to express our individual and collective grief at the loss of someone so young and so active.

It was through his involvement in sport that many of us knew and respected Nigel. In sport, as in everything else, Nigel was a village man through and through. He played soccer for years with Rothley Imps F.C. and was an immensely cultured footballer who always kept a cool head. As a cricketer with Rothley Park C.C., Nigel was outstanding. In 1985 he won the Perkins Shield for the best individual performance of the season. He also won the first X1 Bowling averages. He was undoubtedly good enough to play at a far higher standard of cricket, but that issue never seriously arose because of Nigel's love for the village and its cricket club.

But to focus on sport provides only a glimpse of someone who had so many facets to his personality. His integrity, reliability and conscientiousness always stood out. Even to isolate qualities such as these, however, is to present but a partial picture of Nigel. He was essentially a rounded personality who enjoyed life and who, in the difficult last weeks of his life, showed immense courage.

We also remember Nigel as a loving husband and father. He lived for his family: for Julia and their children Matthew (4), Stuart (2) and Ashley (1). Theirs really was a devoted, caring family. That closeness and devotion makes the pain of death all the more severe.

To Julia and the boys, to all who are nearest and dearest, our deepest sympathy. Nigel was a very special person. To have known him was indeed a privilege.

Dr David Wilson

Chapter 1

Is this the end?

"Grief is the price we pay for love."
(Queen Elizabeth II)[1]

It was late evening, and I was sitting in the chair Nigel always sat in, holding his sweatshirt against my face so I could still smell him. I had decided not to sleep in our bedroom following his unexpected death earlier that morning, as going into the room was so painful and sleeping in our bed all alone was something I simply couldn't face. My world had changed beyond all recognition in a matter of hours.

My mother had insisted that the doctor prescribe me some sleeping tablets. She had placed them on the fireplace and I just kept gazing at them, thinking how easy it would be to take the whole bottle. I glanced across the room at my sisters-in-law, who were both fast asleep on the sofa. I was absolutely devastated and could have ended it all right then. The pain just seemed too much to bear.

Then I heard a voice (which I now know to be God's) say: "What about your little boys? They have already lost their daddy. How could you take their mummy away, too?"

I couldn't. I loved them so much and knew that I had to be there for them. And I couldn't bear the thought of someone else bringing them up. I instantly knew that, whatever I was feeling, they needed me more than ever before, so my life had to go on.

A bit about Nigel

Nigel's parents, Betty and Roland, had welcomed three daughters into the world, and then a little boy came along. His sisters adored Nigel, and after Betty died when he was four, they helped bring him up. Roland's sister, Margaret, and her husband, Frank, regularly had Nigel to stay, and as they had no children of their own, they really spoiled him.

Nigel was a keen footballer and cricketer; in fact, he was a great all-round sportsman. In 1986 he was presented with the Bowler of the Year award by Rothley Cricket Club for his performance the previous season. He could have gone for trials at Leicester City but chose to play football with his friends in the village instead.

He was such a kind, gentle, friendly man. I only ever saw Nigel really lose his temper once, and that was on the football pitch, when he nearly hit someone. I would sometimes get cross with him and start arguing, and he would just sit there. At the end, he would ask if I had finished. It was infuriating at the time, but it always stopped the argument going much further.

Nothing is impossible

Nigel and I had desperately wanted children during the early stages of our marriage, but it just hadn't happened. After two years of tests and operations, we were told we might never have any, and that if we did it could take a long time. We were both devastated, and Nigel blamed himself. He said that if I wanted to leave him and have children with someone else he wouldn't blame me. I told him I loved him and that marriage was for keeps.

We decided that we would perhaps apply to foster in the future and then possibly adopt. We sold our bungalow to help my dad's struggling business and moved in with my parents, opting to blow the money we had left over on a foreign holiday. Having a beautiful home for children we couldn't have at that point didn't seem so important any more.

I wasn't well while we were away, and a friend who was pregnant at the time suggested I might also be expecting. I laughed and told her it wasn't possible, as we couldn't have children. As the holiday wore on she encouraged me to take a pregnancy test, and I eventually agreed. We had to wait all day for the results, and I could hardly believe it when we discovered we were expecting our first child after six long years of trying.

My consultant said that while I had managed to conceive our first child, Matthew, I might not have any more, but it only took me six months to fall pregnant with Stuart, and as soon as we decided we wanted a third, Ashley was on his way! A lesson I learned here was that when people say something is impossible, it doesn't necessarily mean it is!

> *"And looking at them Jesus said to them, 'With people this is impossible, but with God all things are possible"* (Matthew 19:26, NASB).

> *"For nothing will be impossible with God"* (Luke1:37, ESV).

Illness strikes

We had been married for eleven years by the time Nigel became unwell and were so content up to this point. I had always wanted to be married and have lots of children, and I felt this dream had more than been fulfilled.

Looking back, I can see that God had his hand on me even before I knew him properly. We named our first child Matthew, which means "gift of God", and he surely was. All three boys were Nigel's pride and joy. He worked so hard to provide for us all and was very much a hands-on dad.

We didn't have a lot of money at this point, and all we really wanted was to move from our little two-bedroomed terrace to a three-bedroomed house, so our boys didn't all have to sleep in the same room. We finally achieved that and were so excited. We loved our new home and felt settled as soon as we moved in. The boys were really happy, as we had a large garden and a pig farm behind us. The farm was owned by one of Nigel's relatives, so every evening before bath time we would take them to look at the pigs. They really needed a bath after that! It was a lovely summer, and life seemed pretty good.

Nigel had been ill with a virus for about twelve weeks, and it had left him with a really bad cough. He eventually had some tests done, and at first it was thought that he had a form of asthma. After an X-ray he was referred to the Groby Road Hospital in Leicester (now Glenfield Hospital), which had a reputation for being one of the best heart hospitals in the country, so we knew they would find out what was going on. He was admitted for a biopsy on his heart, and after a few days he was sent home, having been given a follow-up appointment ten days later for his results. He still wasn't well, and in fact he appeared to deteriorate, but the doctors told us to wait for his follow-up appointment the following Tuesday.

It was our youngest son Ashley's first birthday the Friday before the follow-up, and we had also organised a family party for the Sunday, as he was being dedicated at our local Baptist church.

The day of Ashley's birthday arrived and Nigel continued to be really poorly, so I phoned the doctor again to arrange for someone to see him. Once again, they asked me to hang on until the Tuesday, so I took the children shopping for the dedication party and arranged a small birthday tea for Ashley.

On the Saturday morning I asked Nigel if he wanted me to cancel the dedication and party because he was still feeling so ill. He wanted me to press ahead, so I carried on with the preparations.

Nigel looked dreadful on the Sunday morning, and he was coughing so much it made him sick several times. I was really concerned that he wouldn't manage to get through the day. I tried to encourage him to stay in bed and suggested we postpone the dedication, but he was adamant that he wanted everything to go ahead as planned.

The minister, Revd Stuart Clarke, was so kind and sensitive to our situation. He explained at the beginning of the service that Nigel was feeling unwell and that if he had to nip out at any point the service would simply resume when he returned. It was so special, as nearly the whole extended family was together for the first time since our wedding day. The service was amazing, and Nigel somehow managed to make it through the whole thing.

Everyone came back to our house for lunch afterwards. It was a glorious day, so we all sat out in the garden. The children were busy playing with their cousins and everyone was having a lovely time. Although Nigel looked tired and unwell, he seemed to be enjoying this time with the family.

The afternoon wore on and people started to leave, but Nigel's dad Roland decided to stay and watch the World Cup Final with us. However, as we watched it, Nigel started to look even worse than he had earlier, so after it had finished and his dad had left, I called the doctor. I was told to wait until Tuesday again.

I became really anxious, fearful and worried at this point because, while I had no idea how seriously ill Nigel was, I knew that he wasn't right and urgently needed to see a doctor.

Nigel had a bad night, and when the children came into the room on the Monday morning he snapped at them. It was then that I knew we couldn't carry on like this. He was never sharp with the children; it simply wasn't in his nature.

I went straight downstairs, called the surgery again and demanded that they send someone as soon as possible. They said they would get a doctor to come out as soon as possible. It was about 7am, so I called my best friend Sian to ask if she would take Matthew to playgroup. I told her the doctor would be arriving before midday, so I would be able to collect him.

We waited all morning for the doctor, who finally arrived at about 1pm. To my great relief, he informed me that Nigel needed to be admitted to hospital straight away. He suggested I could either call an ambulance or take him there myself. I wanted to take him but had hardly any petrol or money to buy more, so I just hoped we had enough to get him there and me back home again. Sian had collected Matthew for me and dropped him home, and I waited until my parents arrived to look after the boys before taking Nigel in.

"You have a very poorly husband"

As soon as we arrived at the hospital, they whisked him off to the ward on a trolley. He was put on a drip and hooked up to a heart monitor. I was crying and wondering what was happening. The nurse said, "No wonder you're upset. You have a very poorly husband here." That was the first time anyone had even hinted that there might be something seriously wrong with him. I stayed for a while but needed to get home for the children, so I reassured Nigel I would be back that night to see him.

I returned later with my sister Suzanne and sat with him, but he wasn't very chatty. Nigel hated hospitals and any sort of illness. Every time a new nurse appeared they would ask how many children we had. It seemed strange, and I kept wondering why they were so interested.

Before I left, the staff nurse said that when I came back the next day for his results, I would need to bring someone with me. I don't know why, but I just kept thinking they were going to tell us we couldn't have any more children. While we would have liked a fourth child, we could have accepted this. We were really happy with our three sons, so I could have coped with this news. I still didn't think it was anything life-threatening at this point.

Nigel's sister Elaine and her husband Sam came with me the next day. Nigel worked with Sam, and we knew he would wonder why Sam wasn't at work, so we agreed to say that he had swapped shifts to avoid any panic on Nigel's part. Visiting time began at 2pm and his appointment was at 2.30pm. We were told that the consultant would come to the ward to see him.

Tea in china cups

We waited and waited for what seemed to be forever, at which point we were brought tea in china teacups. I suddenly remembered our first appointment at the heart hospital. We had met a really nice man who was waiting for a heart transplant and he said, "You know when it's bad news because they bring out the best china and leave you until the end of the clinic. *Oh no!* I thought. *Is that what they're doing? It's obviously going to be bad news.*

I went to find a nurse and said, "Do you know how much longer the consultant will be? I have to go home soon, as I have three children to collect."

Within minutes, the consultant was by the bed. He said, "As we have discussed, Nigel has cardiomyopathy, which means his heart isn't working quickly enough." He explained that there were three options: I can't remember the first now; the second was tablets he had already tried but hadn't worked; and the third was a heart transplant, which they felt was the best way forward. Basically, he had twelve to eighteen months to receive one or he would die.

I was completely stunned, as I had not anticipated this news. At no point had anyone suggested how seriously unwell he might be. I knew he was ill, but not *that* ill! Nigel didn't say a word. I think he was as stunned as I was by this unexpected news. The consultant said someone from the Royal Papworth Hospital would come to see us the following Friday to discuss the way forward, advising us to make suitable childcare arrangements, as we would need to live at the hospital for quite some time.

I didn't know what to do right at that moment, but I knew I needed to get home to my parents and children. Nigel looked tired, so I kissed him goodbye and told him I would be back for evening visiting time. To this day, I still don't know how I walked out of that hospital and back to the car without keeling over.

How can this be happening to us? I asked myself. Nigel and I were happily married, and my parents, who already had more than enough stress in their lives, didn't have to worry about us. Nigel was like a son to them. They loved him. Sometimes I would joke that he was more like their son and I was more like their daughter-in-law. *How am I going to tell them?* I wondered. *Our lives are about to change dramatically. How are we going to manage?*

Who will look after the boys if I need to spend time supporting Nigel at the hospital? We don't have any money. All these thoughts were racing through my mind.

Elaine and I spent the whole journey home crying as Sam drove us back. After telling my parents, who coped remarkably well, I just sat on the sofa hugging Ashley, not knowing what to do next.

Elaine offered to stay the night, so I wasn't on my own. I went to visit Nigel with a friend later that evening, but he didn't really want to talk. I think he was still in complete shock. It had crossed my mind that he might already have known how ill he was, as the hospital staff suggested it had already been discussed and I hadn't always been present when he saw the doctors because I was with the children a lot of the time. However, he assured me that he hadn't known, and seeing how badly he reacted to the news confirmed that he couldn't have been carrying that secret around with him.

I left him to sleep and said I would bring the boys to see him the following day, which was a Wednesday. The nurse said that Nigel and I needed to talk about the transplant and all that it entailed before our appointment at Papworth Hospital on the Friday, so I tried to do that on the Wednesday, but Nigel didn't want to know. Even seeing the boys didn't help to lift his spirits. I returned in the evening, but he still wouldn't discuss it. All he was bothered about was getting rid of the drip he had in his arm. The nurse said it would be off by 10pm, so I tried to reassure him and said I would be back in the morning.

At 10.15pm I phoned the hospital to see how he was and to ask if they had removed the drip. The sister said they had needed to slow the drip down as he was feeling worse. I started to cry and explained that I couldn't get him to talk about the transplant. She was so kind. She told me to go in as soon as I dropped Matthew off at playschool the next morning and she would sit with us and encourage him to discuss it.

The phone call that changed my life

I went to bed exhausted that night, not knowing what the future held. I was awakened by the landline at 3.45am on the Thursday morning and ran down the stairs to answer. It was the hospital, and they asked me to go in straight away. "Is he that bad?" I asked. All they said was I that I needed to come in immediately.

I phoned my sister, as I had no petrol in my car and no money to buy any. I didn't even know if I would get there in time. She picked me up and we got to the hospital in record time. We were asked to wait in a side room while they found the doctor. Crying and anxious to know what was happening, I asked if I could call my minister, Stuart Clarke. Suzanne went off to phone him, and thankfully he came straight away.

The doctor informed me that Nigel had taken a turn for the worse and had become very poorly overnight. We were taken to sit by his bed and the staff started to explain what was happening, but it all went over my head. I couldn't focus properly, as all I could see was my husband lying in the hospital bed with an oxygen mask over his face and tubes everywhere. I could hear the monitor beeping and see the numbers flashing. *Is this really happening?* I could see that my precious husband was fighting for his life.

We sat and talked for a while, and then I asked Stuart if he would pray for Nigel. He took hold of Nigel's hand and mine, then began to pray. After a while, he said "Lord, if it's your will that Nigel should live, we pray that you would give him the strength to fight this illness. But if it's your will that he should be with you in paradise today, we give you permission to take him. Amen."

As he finished saying that prayer, the monitor dropped and Nigel died. His passing was so incredibly peaceful.

The nurses were all crying, as no one had expected him to die. They explained that in the eight hours that had passed, Nigel had lost the twelve to eighteen months he had been expected to live without a transplant. I felt completely numb about what had happened. *What's going to happen to me?* I thought. *My boys need a father. I need a husband!*

It was then that I began to cry uncontrollably. *This can't be happening to me. It must be some kind of nightmare. Surely I'm going to wake up in a minute!*

I was taken out into a side room, where Suzanne and my dad were waiting. I was still crying, and I kept apologising to Dad for giving him something else to worry about.

The nurses brought me some information about what I needed to do next, then asked if I wanted to see Nigel before we left. I went back to say goodbye, knowing my husband would never be coming home with me again. It was so surreal.

Returning home

Pastor Stuart drove me and my dad home on a beautiful summer's day. We were greeted by my sisters-in-law, Ann and Elaine, along with my mum. They all looked at me in disbelief, with tears in their eyes. They tried to make me eat and drink something, but I couldn't. I felt too sick.

Family came and went; it was all a bit of a blur. I remember looking out of the lounge window and seeing Nigel's pyjamas and dressing gown hanging on the line. I had wanted to hold them so I could still sense him with me. *Who washed them?* I ran into the kitchen, where some of my family were sitting. I knew people were just trying to be helpful, but I was so angry and upset about this.

I ran upstairs and hunted through his wardrobe to find something he had worn recently but hadn't been washed and still had his scent on it. Grabbing his favourite sweatshirt, I threw myself onto the bed, sobbing uncontrollably. I had never felt pain like it; it was indescribable. *Why me?* I wondered. *What have I done to deserve this?*

Chapter 2

The days that followed

"The Lord is close to the brokenhearted and saves those
who are crushed in spirit." (Psalm 34:18)

There were so many things to organise after Nigel died. First, I had to go and register his death. Thankfully, Pastor Stuart offered to take me and my dad. I think he realised it was too much for Dad to drive us there and take charge of everything. Back then, you didn't make an appointment the way you would today; you simply turned up and waited.

There were people there waiting to register births and marriages as well as deaths, so we just had to sit around until we were called into the office. The waiting room was dark and gloomy, and it felt as though it was taking forever. When we were eventually invited into the office, the questions asked were horribly direct: "Are you the widow of the deceased?" *Hang on, he's my husband,* I thought. I hated the term 'deceased', and to this day I think it's an awful description.

Once again, I found myself thinking, *This has to be a dream. Surely I'm going to wake up from this nightmare soon.* But once all the forms were finally completed, we received the death certificate. I sobbed uncontrollably again at this point, as seeing it in writing that Nigel was dead made it even more real. My dad looked awful.

He wanted to make everything better for me, and I felt like his little girl again, but he was struggling with his own grief.

I never would have thought it possible for a person to shed as many tears as I had in the short period since Nigel had died. I felt emotionally and physically worn out; as though I was drowning and couldn't do anything about it.

Making arrangements

We went home and set about choosing an undertaker. There was one in the village who Nigel's family knew, so we arranged for him to visit the following day.

The next major decision I had to make was when to tell the boys what had happened to their daddy. I particularly felt for Stuart, as he had gone everywhere with Nigel while he was off sick, as he hadn't been old enough to attend the playgroup. I sensed he would miss his daddy more than the other two because they had spent so much time together.

Matthew and Stuart were both at playgroup that morning because the manager had offered to take Stuart as soon as she heard what had happened. Ashley was asleep upstairs, and I knew I needed to fetch the boys and have them home with me. Several people had offered to collect them, but it was Matthew's last day there as he was heading to primary school that September, so I felt it was really important for me to be there for him, and I wanted life to be as normal as possible for my boys.

It was decided that I would go with Suzanne. I still remember pulling up outside the village hall and getting out of the car. Some of the mums already knew what had happened and several came over to offer their condolences. I had to be strong because I didn't want the boys to know there was anything wrong. As playgroup was breaking up for the summer, they were running late collecting all their things. I was able to cope fairly well so long as I didn't think about what had happened. I went to each member of staff and thanked them for all they had done with Matthew and for having Stuart for the morning. I said we would see them in September, when Stuart was due to start there.

We finally got back into the car. I had somehow managed to keep it together for my three little boys, who had no idea that life would never be the same again. I was so glad I had taken them to see Nigel the previous afternoon.

After discussing it with my parents and in-laws, I had decided not to tell them straight away, mainly because I didn't know how I was going to do it and needed time to think. We returned home for lunch, then arranged for Stuart and Matthew to stay with my parents until the weekend. I wanted to protect them from people coming over and crying, which would have upset them. I needed to keep one of them with me for reassurance, so I kept Ashley, who was too young to know what was going on. We agreed that I would visit my parents at the weekend and tell the children about Nigel then. I had two days to get my head around everything.

The following day I had to go to the bank. My money had been frozen because it was in a joint account. I wanted to go on my own, which didn't go down too well with those around me. I understood that people were trying to be helpful and supportive, and I really appreciated it, but I needed space to do some of the things I had to do on my own.

As I walked down the road into the village, where everybody knew everything about each other, a couple of old ladies I knew crossed the road when they saw me. They obviously knew about Nigel's death but didn't know what to say to me, which is not uncommon when someone dies. I followed them over the road and into the chemist, and grabbed one of their hands. I gently whispered, "It's all right. I'm okay." They just stood there with tears in their eyes.

Nigel had been born in the village and had spent nearly all his life there, so most people knew him. His mother had died when he was four, and the village had rallied round to help his dad cope with three daughters and a son. These ladies had watched Nigel grow up and couldn't understand why he had been taken so young when they had lived so long. They felt it should have been one of them, as Nigel had his whole life ahead of him. I did what I needed to do at the bank, then went home to face more visitors.

The village undertaker was due to visit that afternoon. As he walked slowly down the drive, I noticed he was crying. Bless him. He had never got over losing his son, who had died of cancer as a teenager, and having known Nigel all his life, my husband's death had really got to him. He was so lovely and kind, but he wasn't much use to me at that moment. I was really struggling and needed someone who could take control and help me plan the funeral without becoming an emotional wreck himself!

The arrangements were so expensive, and I felt bad spending so much as Nigel and I had never had much money, though I was very fortunate that the undertaker substantially discounted the funeral. I also found the decision as to whether Nigel should be buried or cremated a really difficult one to make. We had never spoken about death; we had only ever talked about growing old together. I had no idea which he would have wanted. It was all so overwhelming.

I understand now how important it is to let someone know what we want when we die, as it's such a difficult decision for others to make on our behalf, particularly if they are left on their own. If you haven't had this sort of conversation, I would encourage you to do so. Sadly, we will all face these situations one day.

I eventually decided to have his body cremated and bury his ashes in the churchyard two doors down from where we lived. I wanted my boys to have somewhere to go to feel close to him when they grew up if they needed to. That was really important to me, and I knew it would have been to Nigel.

Telling the boys their daddy had died

My brother-in-law Dave offered to drop me at church, then collect me and take me to my parents' house for Sunday lunch. My parents were happy for me to go to church, as they knew it made me feel better.

Our church family was amazing. They made sure someone sat with me and helped me look after Ashley. Pastor Stuart announced Nigel's death to the church that morning. It was very emotional; I could see people were shocked. I cried all the way through the worship. It all felt so surreal, as the last time I had been there our whole extended family, including Nigel, had been there to celebrate Ashley's dedication, and the next time I would be there for his funeral. *How could this be happening to me?* I thought. *When am I going to wake up from this awful nightmare?*

Dave collected me from church and drove me to my parents' house. I was so pleased to see the boys, but as I looked down at their little faces I knew I was about to do the hardest thing I had ever done in my life. We had lunch, then I took them into my parents' lounge and told them their daddy had died and gone to heaven. I can't really remember what I said. It feels as if it were a lifetime ago now, and I don't think they really understood anyway. But I remember feeling as though I was the worst mum in the world, and that I had let them down.

Later that day, the boys and I returned home. My sister-in-law Ann came to stay so she could help me with the children until the day before the funeral. It was important for her to be with her family that night, which I understood. Elaine and her husband Sam and Ann and her husband Dave provided me with such incredible help and support in those early days. I don't think I would have coped without them. We remain close to this day, and I am eternally grateful for everything they did. I have never forgotten the fact that while I had lost my husband and the father of my three boys, they had lost their wonderful and only brother.

Chapel of rest

I wanted to go and see Nigel at the chapel of rest, but I was really scared, as I had given permission for him to have a post-mortem so they could take a sample of his heart for research purposes. I didn't know what to expect, as I had heard some distressing stories, but a friend went to see him first and reassured me that he looked fine, so I visited him with Suzanne, still feeling a little apprehensive.

I remember walking into the room and all I could see were his feet, which looked enormous! I had given the undertaker Nigel's best clothes and shoes. It was fashionable in those days to wear wedge shoes, so his feet looked bigger than usual. I glanced up to see his face, and I wanted to touch him as his hair hadn't been done the way he usually had it. I so wanted to put it right, but Suzanne wouldn't let me. I think she felt uncomfortable about me touching him.

I had brought some roses from our front garden for him, which I placed on his chest. I felt like I was in a daze; it just didn't feel like this was my life at all. This wasn't *my* Nigel. I just wanted him to come back and for everything to return to normal.

A friend suggested it was perhaps a blessing that Nigel had died because it meant he wasn't suffering any more. I was so upset;

I just couldn't see it like that. I would have wanted him there even if he had needed twenty-four-hour care. I loved him and would have been there for him whatever the situation. I realised later on he would have hated it, and that I was being a bit selfish, but it's how I felt at the time.

The funeral

The funeral was due to take place exactly a week after the day Nigel died. The time flew by, as there was so much to do and a constant stream of visitors offering their condolences. Much of it is still a blur.

I needed to buy something suitable to wear. In those days it was traditional to wear mainly black for a funeral. It was incredibly hard, as I wanted to look like me for Nigel's sake, but all the black clothes I tried on made me look awful. I don't know how many outfits I tried on. When the sales assistants realised it was for my husband's funeral they didn't know what to say. I felt so sorry for them. In the end I wore a dress that had some black in it. I had bought it for Christmas and worn it for Ashley's dedication, so I knew Nigel liked it.

I was very close to my cousin Christine and her husband Harry, so I asked if they would come to stay the night before the funeral and support me on the day. I felt it would be too much for my parents, who were struggling to hold it together. When I woke up that morning – a beautiful, sunny July day – I felt physically sick. They encouraged me to eat something, but all I had really eaten since that dreadful day was dry toast. That was all I could really face. I just felt overwhelmed by everything.

When I put on my dress, I realised I had lost a lot of weight. It was hanging off me. I had been trying to lose weight for years, but this certainly wasn't the way I had wanted to achieve it.

I would have loved to have one of the boys there to sit on my knee and cuddle, but children didn't go to funerals in those days. A friend from church had Ashley and the older boys went to my neighbours, who had lost a child a few years earlier. I knew they would all be in safe hands.

I felt so lost and alone as we waited for the hearse to arrive. I looked out of the window in disbelief when it eventually came. *This can't be happening*, I thought to myself. I rushed to the bathroom and was physically sick. *How am I going to get through the next few hours, let alone the rest of my life?* My life as I knew it was over. I felt I had nothing to look forward to ever again.

I walked down the drive to the hearse and stopped to look at the coffin my husband – the man I loved with all my heart – was lying in. I was heartbroken. *Please let me wake up!* I cried out silently in my head. *This can't be my life!*

Nigel and I had made so many plans for our future. We had joked about walking to collect our pensions from the village post office, wondering how we would manage, given that we lived at the top of a hill. We had figured we could roll down but it would have been a nightmare to get back up! I had never for a moment imagined that we wouldn't grow old together.

I got into the funeral car with Christine, Harry and my parents. My parents looked awful. They were so worried about me, and I just wanted to make them feel better.

When the car pulled up at the church, it looked as if half the village had turned out. People were standing outside the church and even across the road. Many of them were crying and others looked shocked or in a state of disbelief. Nigel had been incredibly popular and well known in the village.

I remember walking into the church behind Nigel's coffin, and all I could hear was people sobbing. The whole building, including the balcony, was completely packed. I wanted to scream,

This is so unfair! Why me?! Why us? There were many elderly people in our family, and they had all said that it should have been one of them instead. Right then I was thinking, *Yes, it should have been. Nigel had everything to live for.*

The service began, and as we started to sing the tears came uncontrollably. People got up and gave tributes, and it all just felt like a dream. Pastor Stuart was brilliant. He had come back from his holiday early to take the funeral, for which I will be forever grateful. He had visited Nigel several times at home and also during the few days Nigel was in hospital to talk with and pray for him, and he was convinced that Nigel had given his life to Jesus the day before he died. Pastor Stuart had left Nigel a "Journey into Life" tract to read, which explained the gospel clearly.

After the church service we headed to the crematorium in Loughborough. It was there that I remember getting out of my seat, going to touch the coffin and completely breaking down. I just sobbed and sobbed when the curtain was drawn and it disappeared from sight. *What am I going to do?* I asked myself. I felt completely alone in the world. I knew my life would never be the same.

I have no recollection of who I talked to after the service. Again, it was a complete blur. I just knew that I wanted to get my children back as soon as possible. I needed them more than ever before.

We returned to our house for the wake, and one thing I clearly remember is my mum being really upset because the sandwiches were like doorsteps! The undertaker's wife had done the spread free of charge to keep my costs down, bless her. I loved my mum dearly, but she could be a bit of a snob at times. She would have taken the crusts off and cut them into four neat triangles if she had done the spread. I found her in the kitchen cutting the sandwiches in half to make them look a bit daintier. Years later we all laughed about it, and she definitely saw the funny side.

Sandwiches aside, I truly felt as though my life was over that day. You may have experienced a similar day in your life. A day when you felt that life as you once knew it had ended forever. However, I soon discovered that God is able to rescue, restore and rebuild broken lives. He is more than able to do the same for you, so please don't lose hope. Put your trust in Father God.

Chapter 3

Facing life alone

"...Never will I leave you; never will I forsake you." (Hebrews 13:5)

As people began to leave after the wake, Elaine offered to stay with me. I replied that I would have to be on my own eventually, so I might as well start from then. It wasn't something I wanted to do, but it had to be done. I couldn't expect Ann or Elaine to stay with me forever, as they both had families to care for and needed to deal with their own grief. It was time for me to start facing life without Nigel.

The house gradually emptied, and then it was just me and the boys. By six o'clock they were all ready for bed and went straight to sleep. I was so glad that Nigel and I had them in a solid routine and that I hadn't allowed what had happened to change it too much. They had always been exceptionally good little boys.

In *Living with Grief*, Esther Rantzen said that "loneliness is weird".[2] She had read a newspaper article in which someone defined loneliness as having plenty of people to do something with but nobody to do nothing with. This really resonated with me.

I was properly alone that night for the first time since Nigel had died. I had always been afraid of being on my own, and I didn't like it at all. I so missed the companionship of being a couple and the security of Nigel looking after me. There I was, all alone and solely responsible for three young children, and I found myself beginning to feel anxious and fearful. *What if something happens in the night? What if we have a fire? How will I get them all out? Who will I rescue first?* All these thoughts started whirling around in my head.

Exhausted from the day, I eventually went to bed at about 9pm, but I couldn't sleep because I felt so scared and lonely. I could hear every little creak in the house. I still remember babysitting for people when I was sixteen and being absolutely petrified at every little sound, wishing the parents would come home early.

I eventually got up and opened my bedroom curtains slightly. There was a street light directly outside, which meant I was no longer in the dark. I pulled the quilt over my head and started to sob as quietly as I could so as not to disturb the boys. Knowing we would never be together again as a family was too painful to think about. It made me feel as if I'd had the stuffing knocked out of me.

The night seemed endless as I tossed and turned, drifting in and out of sleep. I eventually woke up at about 7.30am and lay there thinking to myself, *What's the point of getting up? My life is over.* Suddenly I heard a shout from one of the bedrooms: "Mum, I want my breakfast!" I had to get up because my boys needed me more than ever! They gave me a purpose; a reason to get myself up and carry on with my life.

Feeling numb and suffocated

The days that followed were like a horrible dream. I was still in shock and felt completely numb. Life just didn't seem real. I would enter a room but feel as if I wasn't really there. My grief was raw and very painful; nothing like any sadness I had experienced before. I didn't know what I wanted from one day to the next, and I felt as if I didn't belong anywhere.

I was invited out for meals with the children but felt awkward as my friends' husbands would be there and I didn't have one any more. Apparently, this is not unusual for those who lose a partner. It's common to feel uncomfortable or as though you are the odd one out. Worse still, one of the husbands, whose marriage was struggling, made me feel really uneasy because he kept flirting with me.

I also felt as if I was being suffocated by my own and Nigel's family. It felt as if they were checking up on me all the time, which was quite understandable as they loved me and were worried about me and the boys, but it made me feel swamped at times.

Both sides of the family were incredible – in fact, I don't know what I would have done without them – but they were coping with their own grief, and I don't think I understood them or they me. I have since discovered that this is absolutely normal, as we all grieve differently. There is no magic formula.

Feeling isolated

As the days went by, I felt incredibly isolated, as though I was living in a void. Yes, I had three wonderful little boys who gave me a reason to live and kept me company, but I missed Nigel desperately. The harsh reality was that he would never walk through the front door again. We would never discuss our days or make plans for the future. I would never again feel his arms around me or the touch of his lips on mine.

I had lost my companion and soulmate. Nigel was the person I always went home to, and he was no longer there. My whole life was impacted by his death. I had shared so many precious memories with him; both sad and joyful. We had made plans for the future. He was a part of me. He knew what made me tick and how I felt about things. He was my comfort and support.

Sometimes it took every bit of strength within me just to get out of bed in the morning, let alone get through the day. I missed adult interaction so much, as I spent some days solely with the boys and never spoke to another adult. We didn't have FaceTime, WhatsApp or Skype calls back then; all we had was a landline. There was no social media to keep me in touch with other people's lives. I felt so alone.

Wine became my crutch

Matthew started school that September, just two months after Nigel died, and after I had collected him and closed the front door at around 4pm, I rarely saw another adult. The boys went to bed at 6pm, so my evenings felt as though they were never-ending. I started having a glass of wine once they were settled to help me relax and forget that my whole world had just fallen apart. Before long, one glass became two or three, and eventually I was putting seven bottles into my trolley when I went to the supermarket each Friday.

One day at about 4pm, I thought to myself, *I wish it was the boys' bedtime now so I could have a drink*. It was then that I realised I would soon have a serious problem if I carried on drinking like that. My boys needed a sober mum, so from that day on I stopped putting wine in my shopping trolley. It's so easy for alcohol to become a crutch if we use it to make a specific situation or aspect of our lives more bearable. It can help to numb the pain for a time, but it isn't the solution.

One day I met with Pastor Stuart, who told me about a lady in the church whose husband had just left her. I said that I wished

I was her. That way, Nigel would only have left me and I would at least have had a hope that he would come back one day. He explained that the lady concerned had said she wished she was me and that her husband had died. That way, she wouldn't have felt so rejected.

Rejection

But I also felt as though I had been rejected somehow. This doesn't really make sense, on reflection, as Nigel hadn't chosen to leave me. I suspect this is a common emotion for those who have lost a loved one, no matter how irrational it seems. Author Maria Kubitz writes: "Intense grief can make the irrational seem rational."[3]

I recently watched a series called *Virgin River*, in which the lead actress suggested that grief is circular. I have found this to be true, and it often hits me when I least expect it. I can be fine one moment and then something happens – a memory, a song or a person suddenly triggers that grief – and it's the most overwhelming feeling. I recently read that you can't control it – it controls you – and I have definitely found that to be the case.

Each special date, such as a birthday or an anniversary, is a fresh challenge, particularly the first time around. *How will I feel?* I wondered. *How will I cope?* I approached each occasion in fear and trepidation of what they might bring, but the feeling of dread was always worse than the actual day.

The dreaded first-year anniversary was horrible, but I found the following day more painful. All through the first year, I could say, "This time last year...", but from that day onwards I wasn't able to say that. It felt as if I was moving further and further away from Nigel. In fact, I found the grief much harder to deal with during the second year.

By the time you reach the end of the first year, many people presume you have got over your loved one's death. That is not the case. There isn't a time limit on grief, and there aren't any rules for dealing with it. Everyone is different. I don't believe we ever fully recover from the loss of a loved one. However, if we allow him in, God will help us come to terms with and live with the loss we have experienced.

Never the same again

My mother was quite cross with me one day when I visited her a few months after Nigel's death. She said I had changed and that I wasn't the person I had been before Nigel died. My response was that she was right. My whole life had changed, and all my hopes and dreams had evaporated overnight. The man I had planned to spend the rest of my life with had died and I was on my own. Why would I have been the same?

Let's Talk About Loss recently posted a picture on Instagram that echoed this sentiment: "One thing we want you to understand about grief: that we won't be the same person we were before they died and nor would we want to be."[4]

Denial

I still recall expecting Nigel to come in from work for the first few months. I also found myself looking for him in the supermarket when I went shopping, and some men actually looked like him if I squinted. I would lie in bed at night pretending he was by my side, holding the pillow as if it were him. I felt so incredibly lonely.

I had no one to hold me; no one to tell me they loved me or to approve of the new dress I was wearing. Matthew must have overheard me telling a friend that I didn't have anyone to tell me

I looked nice when I got ready, as one day while I was getting ready, he said, "Mummy, you look lovely in that dress." I could have cried. He had only just turned five, and suddenly he was growing up.

God held me

As I reflect back over this time, I know that God was holding me in the palm of his hand, and that he never left my side. He formed me and knew me. Better still, I realise now that he had a perfect plan to bring hope and restoration to me and my little boys.

> *Oh yes, you shaped me first inside, then out;*
> *you formed me in my mother's womb.*
> *I thank you, High God – you're breathtaking!*
> *Body and soul, I am marvelously made!*
> *I worship in adoration – what a creation!*
> *You know me inside and out,*
> *you know every bone in my body;*
> *You know exactly how I was made, bit by bit,*
> *how I was sculpted from nothing into something.*
> *Like an open book, you watched me grow from conception to birth;*
> *all the stages of my life were spread out before you,*
> *The days of my life all prepared*
> *before I'd even lived one day.*
> (Psalm 139:13-16, MSG)

Thankful in loss

During my journey to faith, a Christian friend took me to a coffee morning where a lady shared about the loss of her baby. I remember her saying that her child had lived for just three days, and that she thanked God for those precious moments. She said those three days were so special and that she had treasured every minute with her daughter, as some people were unable to have a child or spend any time with them.

This made me realise how fortunate I was to have been married to Nigel for more than eleven years and to have enjoyed six precious years with him before the children arrived. I was desperate to have a baby from the day we got married, but when I reflected on it I was so thankful to God that we had been given that time to really get to know one another and make some fantastic memories together. I regularly thanked God for that, as I might never have had that quality time with him if we had conceived straight away.

Creating some sense of "normality"

My family encouraged me to start returning to normality, so I joined a basket-weaving class at a local night school while a relative babysat for me. It did me the world of good to get out of the house, and I really began to enjoy it. I made friends and was soon invited to join some of the girls at our local pub.

After a couple of weeks, the family member who was babysitting remarked that she didn't think it was right for me to go to the pub as a young widow because of what people might say, and she refused to sit for me again. When I said that my father-in-law, who had lost his wife and been left with a young family, had regularly gone to the pub, she replied that it was acceptable for a man but not for a woman. I was furious, as I wasn't doing anything wrong. I was just trying to enjoy some much needed 'me time'. I was fortunate in that I had the means to pay a babysitter my friend had recommended by this time, and it was much better than relying on family all the time.

This was a really tough season in my life, and at times I felt like the whole village was watching me. It seemed as though everyone was discussing my life and any choices I made for myself and my family. It felt like I was under a massive microscope, and I just couldn't please everyone. Everyone seemed to have an opinion on how I should move forward with my life. People say they understand, but they don't. How could they? They weren't walking in my shoes.

How God helped me through this season of loneliness

One thing I discovered during this time was that God was always there for me. I read relevant scriptures that members of my church family had said would bring me comfort. I talked to God and told him exactly how I felt, which really helped me get it off my chest. Sometimes I cried and shouted at him, but I knew he understood. Although I didn't know God very well back then, and certainly didn't understand the season I was going through, I always sensed his presence and knew he was with me. There were days when I particularly felt his strength helping and carrying me through.

The Bible promises that if we draw near to God, he will draw near to us (see James 4:8). This was certainly my experience. In perhaps the most famous psalm every written, David declared:

> *"Even though I walk through the valley of the shadow of death, I will fear no evil, for you are with me; your rod and your staff, they comfort me"* (Psalm 23:4, ESV).

I was given a card with the well-known "Footprints in the Sand" poem[5] on by a friend, and that really helped me understand how well God would look after me and that even during the darkest

31

and most challenging times of my life, he was not only walking by my side but carrying me.

This poem may be familiar to you, but I want to encourage you to really grasp the fact that God is with you though the storms of life. There are certainly times when we should jump into his strong, loving arms and allow him to carry us.

God promises in the Bible that he will never leave or abandon us. I felt very alone at this time, and you may well feel alone in your grief, but one thing I discovered during this dark season was that God never abandons his children. He is a good Father. He is *your* good Father.

Chapter 4

Finding Christ

"It's in Christ that we find out who we are and what we are living for. Long before we first heard of Christ and got our hopes up, he had his eye on us, had designs on us for glorious living, part of the overall purpose he is working out in everything and everyone."
(Ephesians 1:11-12, MSG)

Growing up, I always believed there was a God but had no idea that I could have a personal relationship with him. Like many people, I had gone to church with my parents for christenings, weddings and funerals, and a neighbour we called 'auntie' took us to the harvest festival at her church every year. I loved going with her, as she used to make us the most amazing baskets of fruit and vegetables to take to the altar, but I was never particularly interested in the faith aspect.

We had to go to church every Sunday morning while I was at boarding school. We were marched through the centre of Loughborough to the Church of England church in our Sunday uniform. To say that I found it boring would be a huge understatement! I felt like we were on show, as everyone in the town knew where we went to school. We had to be on our best behaviour, and I wasn't really the best-behaved pupil during that period!

Despite this, I prayed every night before I went to sleep for as long as I can remember that God would keep me and my family safe. I'm pretty sure that each one of us has an awareness of God even before we discover him for ourselves. It certainly became clear to me that God had already been at work in my life and was drawing me towards him before Nigel died.

Christening

I married Nigel at St Mary & St John in Rothley because I had always wanted a church wedding. As it was a Church of England church, people weren't allowed to have their children christened there unless they were regular attendees or promised to attend regularly. I knew quite a few people who made that promise and never set foot in the church after the christening. I refused to make a promise I knew I wouldn't be able to keep, so I had the eldest two christened at a church in nearby Cossington.

When I asked to have Ashley christened at the same church they said no, as we were outside the Cossington parish area and the previous vicar had retired. I was furious, and I remember rambling on about it for weeks! It just didn't sound very Christian to me.

Not long after Ashley was born, my friend and neighbour, Sian, invited me and the boys to a weekly coffee morning at the local Baptist church. I loved going with Sian and meeting so many new people. The church provided us with really cheap lunches and there were lots of toys for the children to play with. It became the highlight of my week because there weren't many places I could afford to take the boys for lunch at that time and also have some adult conversation.

Nearly a tragedy!

We were taking Matt to playschool one day, and I had pushed the pram, with Ashley in it, out of the gate at the side of our house. I turned to shut the gate behind me, trapping Stuart's finger as I did so! Horrified, I let go of the pram to help him, and it rolled down the steep slope into the road. It even tipped upside down. I was hysterical because I had noticed a car at the top of the hill heading in our direction. Fortunately, the driver had seen what was happening and slowed down.

I ran out into the road. The boys were screaming and Ashley was hanging upside down in the pram. He was only a few weeks old and didn't really need a harness, but for some unknown reason I had strapped him in that morning. I can't imagine what might have happened if he had been thrown out of the pram at that age. Hearing the disturbance below her house, Sian came rushing down and took me inside to calm me down. All I remember was screaming that he wouldn't have gone to heaven if he had died as he hadn't been christened.

The following Friday we were talking about this near miss at the coffee morning. I was still traumatised, genuinely believing that if Ashley had been killed, he wouldn't have gone to heaven. The minister's wife, June, said something to me that had a massive impact on my life: "What sort of God do you think we worship that would send a baby to hell?" It was quite a revelation to me, and it helped me understand God better.

We also discussed Ashley's christening and June informed me that I could have Ashley dedicated at the church. I explained that I couldn't because I was "C of E" (Church of England). Looking back, it was so funny how our family always said this. Although we didn't attend church, my parents had brought us up with quite high moral standards. For instance, we were never allowed to blaspheme and got a whack around the head if we did! My dad had attended boarding school for years and been forced to attend church three times every Sunday, so he knew quite a lot of scripture. I am convinced to this day that he had a faith of some sort.

June invited me to church almost every week. Each time she asked I would agree to attend, but then I never went. She eventually wore me down because I felt really bad for not going, so I finally decided to give it a try.

It's worth pointing out that if someone had just arranged to take me, I would have gone a lot earlier. It was the thought of going on my own that put me off. Also, if you have friends who say no when you invite them, don't stop asking. June never gave up on me, and I'm totally convinced that I wouldn't have gone at that time if she had.

I woke the boys up early that Sunday morning and got them ready. Nigel was working at the Walkers crisps factory, so I prepared the Sunday lunch to be ready for when he got home. I was so nervous that I was in and out the bathroom all morning. We nearly didn't go, as I had no idea what to expect. *Where will I put the pram?* I wondered. *What will happen with the boys?*

I arrived early and was led over to a seat near the kitchen so the pram could be tucked away but I could still keep an eye on Ashley while he was asleep. I loved the whole service from beginning to end. The people were so welcoming and nice to us all, and from that day on I hardly missed a Sunday.

What would you say if I became a Christian?

It was the first Christmas after I started attending church that Nigel started to become unwell. It began with a virus that left him with a lingering cough. He eventually went back to work for a while but had to return home on sick leave after a couple of weeks. One of his duties involved climbing a high tower to make sure the smell of crisps didn't spread too far. One day he felt quite dizzy while he was doing it, so he was sent home. That turned out to be his last ever day at work.

Approximately six weeks before Nigel died, we were lying in bed and I remember saying to him, "What would you say if I became a Christian?" I didn't really know what a Christian was at the time. Pastor Stuart preached a gospel message once a month at the family service, but they never really resonated with me. I presume I just wasn't ready for it at that time.

Nigel said it was fine with him as long as I didn't expect him to go to church as well. As I lay in bed, I shut my eyes and said, "God, if you are real, I am yours." I never gave it much more thought until after Nigel died.

I couldn't put my finger on it, but I knew these people had something I didn't. Later, when they heard that Nigel was ill, they started praying for him. Pastor Stuart even offered to come over and pray with him, and to my surprise Nigel agreed.

I remember listening to an afternoon chat show around this time in which pop star Alvin Stardust was sharing how he became a Christian. Again, I was intrigued and wanted what he had, but I just didn't know how to get it.

We decided to have Ashley dedicated after Stuart's visit. He explained that dedication was an opportunity to thank God for the children and the whole family, and to dedicate them all to God, but made it clear that it was not a guarantee of salvation. He added that Ashley was too young to make a decision of his own but would be able to do so when he was old enough to understand.

It all seemed to make sense, so we started making plans. We were in the process of moving house at the time, so we decided to hold the dedication a few weeks later, which we hoped would give Nigel time to get better.

The cross on the wardrobe door

I really wanted to become a Christian after Nigel's death, but I knew my family would think that I wasn't in my right mind. I had been reading Cliff Richard's book, *Power for Living*, repeatedly, as I was fascinated by the way he had come to know Christ. In the middle was the prayer of salvation, which I always skipped so I could carry on reading. I just hadn't been sure that I was ready to make that commitment.

I started going to a house group at the church after he died, and one night I came home and got into bed. As I looked at the wardrobe where Nigel had kept his clothes, I saw the reflection of the window frame on the wardrobe door. It looked just like a cross. I knew in that moment that I couldn't go through life on my own any more. I immediately picked up Cliff's book and read the prayer out loud.

I didn't feel any different, so I read it out again and again, but I still didn't feel any change. I didn't really know what I was expecting to happen. A flash of lights? An earthquake? A thunderous voice? There was nothing at all, so I went to sleep. That was on 2nd October 1986.

I realise now that I became a Christian at that moment because Jesus said:

"I will never turn away anyone who comes to me" (John 6:37, GNT).

Introducing Simon

I didn't tell anyone about the decision I had made, but the following Saturday morning the local churches were taking part in a March for Jesus between the two adjoining villages of Rothley and Mountsorrel. When it finished, I returned home alone with the boys.

I was out the front of my house gardening that afternoon when Simon rode by on his bicycle. I knew Simon from the Baptist church, where he was serving as a student assistant minister. Nowadays he would have been called an intern. He was planning to study at Spurgeon's College in London that year to become a Baptist minister. Simon had met Nigel a few weeks before he died – once at the village fete and also on the days when he brought Matt home from Boys' Brigade, where he was a leader.

Simon was on his way to see his fiancée, but he stopped to talk. I told him I had prayed the prayer of salvation earlier in the week. He said he had thought there was something different about me at the march that morning. He told me to put the kettle on so I could tell him all about it. Then he encouraged me to tell people at church on Sunday, as many of them had been praying for me to find Jesus. We talked for ages and he answered loads of my questions.

A lady welcomed me as I arrived at church with the boys the next Sunday, and I told her I had given my life to Jesus. She was so pleased. I later found out that she was Simon's mum, Janet, and that she and two other ladies had been praying for me every week.

Finding Jesus is the best thing that has ever happened to me. He transformed my life in ways I never could have imagined.

It didn't change dramatically overnight, but knowing I wasn't alone on this journey any more made me feel much stronger. Being a Christian doesn't make all the tough things go away, but it gave me an incredible and unexplainable peace. Knowing that Jesus is there every minute of every day, helping, guiding and providing for me, has made me more determined to make the most of the life he had given me.

Chapter 5

Moving forward

"I have learned that life is a considerable gift and to be given two chances at it means it has to be a God-given gift."
(Desmond Wilcox)[6]

A friend came to visit me with her sister the day after Nigel died, and I'll never forget her words when I told her my life was over: "Don't worry, you'll meet somebody else."

What?! I thought to myself. *You've got to be joking! My husband has literally just died. I don't want to meet anyone else!* I didn't say anything, but I felt so hurt that she thought it was even an option. All I could imagine was growing old on my own. The future looked awful.

I don't think she meant to hurt me; she just wanted to help me see that I had a future. People can say really careless things when they don't know how to help, and I have discovered that people are often lost for words when someone dies. They just want to make you feel better, yet they simply don't know how.

I always say to people that they don't need to say anything when somebody dies. It's better to just be there for the person who is grieving. Hold their hand, cry with them, support them. Do something nice. Let them know they aren't forgotten. In the early days, people say they will be there for you, and some of them are.

But as time goes by they will simply get on with their own lives, which is natural and understandable. It's at this point that you begin to realise how alone you are.

It's also really hard to ask people for help. I had a young couple called Russell and Lorraine move in next door to me not long after Nigel died. They were amazing neighbours. They regularly took the boys out and cooked tea for us. Some nights I would pass the boys over the garden wall and they would bath them and get them ready for bed, then pass them back. The boys loved spending time with them. They had so much fun.

People like that were invaluable because I also found that I needed time to myself; time to get my thoughts together. One of Simon's friends, Dave, also took them out in his car for me. One day he took Matthew shopping and placed a dozen eggs on the rear parcel shelf of his car. On the way home he had to slam the brakes on and the eggs flew off the shelf and smashed, with some of the yolk landing on Matthew. Dave looked really nervous when they arrived on my driveway and explained what had happened. I think he was scared that I would react badly, but I saw the funny side… and Dave was left to clean his car up!

Protecting myself from being hurt again

When I was sixteen, I had been going out with a boy for more than a year when he suddenly dumped me. I was devastated, as I thought he was destined to be the love of my life. I vowed I would never let that happen again, so whenever I met anyone who wanted to get serious I would quickly get out of the relationship. I have to say that I wasn't very nice, and I treated one guy in particular very badly. I just didn't want to get hurt again.

But then I met Nigel when I was eighteen. We met in the September, got engaged in the December and married the following

June. People said we were too young and that we should wait, but I'm so glad we didn't listen to them and went ahead with it. A friend of my dad had said at the time that Nigel wasn't good enough for me, but while Nigel was in hospital, he came and apologised. He had realised by then what a lovely, kind, gentle man Nigel was. In fact, when Nigel died, he said he wished it could have been him instead, as he had already enjoyed a good life.

Simon had started visiting me regularly as part of his role, and one day I told him how hard I found it to take the boys out for the day on my own. He said he would be more than willing to come along and help out, and a few days later we found ourselves at Twycross Zoo in Leicestershire. We had a lovely time, although it felt a bit awkward when we bumped into someone from church. By the end of the day, I had realised there was something more than friendship there. I felt awful that I might actually have feelings for someone else so soon after Nigel's death.

I pushed my emotions to one side and tried not to think about Simon. I still loved Nigel with all my heart, and I felt as though I was betraying him by meeting someone else so quickly. I have since read that it's quite common for people who had been in a really happy relationship when their partner died to meet someone else and want to get married, as their past experience had been a good one. Conversely, those who had been in unhappy relationships usually wouldn't want to jump into another in case history repeated itself.

Starting again

So there I was, thinking about starting all over again with someone new. *How am I going to tell my family and friends?* I asked myself. *More importantly, how am I going to tell Nigel's family?* I felt dreadful. I didn't eat much during this period, as I was never really hungry and often felt sick. I recognise now that this was the shock. It's the only time in my adult life that I have ever been a size eight! My parents were worried that I wasn't eating and would send meals for me, but I just wasn't hungry – the grief made me feel physically sick. However, I always made sure the boys were well fed.

One evening Simon invited himself over for a meal. His excuse was that he wanted to encourage me to eat a proper meal. He bought me a book, which I still have to this day. Inside it says:

To Julia,
Welcome to God's family.
I hope this will help you hang on in there!
Simon

Helping an old lady across the road

Simon invited me to the cinema to see *Top Gun* for our first date. I was like a nervous teenager, as I had forgotten how it felt to date someone new. We sat through the film, side by side but not touching. Then on our way home, Simon suggested going for a drink. We parked up over the road from a village pub, and as we crossed over, he grabbed my hand and said, "Can I help an old lady across the road?" That has to be the worst chat-up line ever!

I took the boys to stay with my cousin Christine in Stockport the following weekend. She was always good to me, and had said that I could visit any time I needed to get away. Simon and I had decided not to tell anyone we were dating until things settled down. I'm not sure that ever would have happened in reality, and there was never going to be a good time to break the news. Anyway, I didn't tell Christine, but I still felt like a teenager. I couldn't stop talking about him and he phoned me twice during the two days we were there. We only had landlines in those days, so it wasn't very private. She said later that she knew something was going on.

I was still at Christine's when Simon called me on the Sunday evening to say he had told one of the church leaders about us. I was absolutely mortified, as we had agreed not to say anything. "Why did you do that?" I asked. He explained that he hadn't been able to help it; he had just wanted to tell someone so badly.

On reflection I understand this, as when you start to fall in love with someone they take over your thoughts. You just want to talk about them and tell people how you're feeling. This leader told Simon he was on the rebound because he and his fiancée had recently decided to part ways, and that I didn't know my own mind because I was still grieving.

It was a difficult time for me, because all the 'experts' say you shouldn't make any major decisions within the first twelve months of being widowed. I totally understand that, as one day I thought I wanted one thing and the next day I wanted something else. Yet here I was falling in love with someone in the midst of my bereavement, with three little boys and two concerned families close at hand.

I returned home to discover that a rumour had started going around the church that we were an item. The following Sunday we heard that a couple Simon knew really well had decided not to come to church that week because they felt they couldn't sit behind us. I was shocked that so-called Christians were acting that way, but I realise now that people respond in all kinds of different ways, and often they think they know what's best for others in these situations. This is just one of the many challenges people face when they lose their spouse and start dating again. It's not easy.

Prayer and cream cakes

Simon came to see me the following week and said he needed to go away for three days to pray about our relationship. He said he had lost his peace at church and felt uncomfortable. We agreed that he should go, but I felt so upset after he left. I remember writing in my notebook that if he thought he could just swan back into my life after three days he could forget it! *He* might be able to go away and pray to Jesus about it, but that wouldn't work for *me*. As well as being upset, I was fuming with him. One minute we were together, the next we weren't. *Who does he think he is, messing with my head like that?* I asked myself.

There was a Nick Berry song at the time that resonated with me. It talked about a couple who had nearly made it, but then decided they must have read the signs incorrectly and that whatever they once had was all gone. I recorded it on *Top of the Pops* and kept replaying it and crying all evening. I really believed it was over and felt even worse than I had before we started going out.

The following morning there was a knock at the door and Simon was standing there with some cream cakes. We laugh about it now, but he had no idea just how close he was to getting them rammed down the back of his throat! He had realised by this point that it wasn't his peace with God he had lost, but other people pressuring him that had made him feel bad. He wanted to carry on seeing me.

However, he suggested that for the boys' sakes we needed to pray and ask God if there was a future for us. They had already lost Nigel and Simon didn't think it was fair for them to spend a lot of time with him if we didn't have a future together, as they would be left on their own again. I freaked out a bit when it came to praying about whether we should get married, as we had only just started going out. But I totally agreed with him about the boys.

This was the first time I ever asked God what I should do next in my life. I was still a baby Christian and didn't know how God spoke to people, so I had to trust Simon that he had heard from God about our relationship.

The following week, Simon visited me in the evening. I had received a few phone calls that day, so I decided to take the phone off the hook for some peace and quiet. A couple of hours later there was a knock at the door. It was Nigel's sister Ann and her husband Dave. They were worried I had done something stupid because they hadn't been able to get hold of me. In hindsight, I would have done the same thing if the roles had been reversed.

They didn't look at all impressed when they came in and saw Simon there, which was understandable. It was so awkward, I just wanted the ground to open and swallow me up! I knew then that life was going to be even more difficult than I had anticipated if we continued seeing each other. I knew people were only thinking of me and the boys, but I knew it was going to be difficult for all of us to move forward.

Getting engaged

Simon said he would either propose somewhere really stupid or somewhere really romantic. Every time we went into the countryside I thought, *This will be it*. He actually did propose to me somewhere really stupid, but that remains between me and him!

He officially proposed to me on the beach at Benllech Bay. He popped the question by writing it in the sand, and I replied, "Yes." A date was set with the help of Pastor Stuart. We told Simon's parents, who were absolutely delighted, and my neighbours Russell and Lorraine, who helped us plan the day.

I really just wanted a quiet wedding and would have been happy to go in through the back door of the church so no one would see me. But Simon said he wanted to celebrate our wedding properly before God and show me off.

We made all the arrangements in secret, as we were concerned that I would receive some criticism once it was out there, and that people would try to talk me out of it. I even remember going into Leicester to order our wedding invitations and asking the assistant if we could do it at the back of the shop in case anyone we knew walked past and saw us.

The big announcement

Simon and I told the boys we were going to get married before we told anyone else. They were really excited and couldn't wait for Simon to come and live with us.

Everything was planned, and six weeks before our wedding day we held a barbecue at my house. We spoke to my parents and Nigel's family about our plans beforehand. Roland said he was okay with it as long as we didn't change the boys' surname, as they were the last of the Toone family to carry it on.

My parents, on the other hand, thought I had lost my mind! As far as they were concerned, Simon didn't have much going for him. He was younger than me and training to be a minister. He had no money or job; in fact, the only thing he owned was a part-share in a second-hand bicycle!

My mother told me I was just trying to replace Nigel, but I wasn't. Nigel was unique! He could never have been replaced, and I didn't want to replace him with anyone else. She also said to me, "You can't be a vicar's wife. You don't like old people!" She clearly had a strange perception of ministry because it involves people of all ages. Besides, I don't ever remember disliking the elderly. Some of my favourite memories are of moments shared with older people!

At the barbecue, Simon's best man John announced that we were engaged to be married, and then handed out the invites. There was quite a mixed reaction. One of my friends walked out crying, but the members of our church family present were thrilled! Some of Simon's friends thought he had lost the plot. *Why would he want to marry someone with three children?* they wondered.

It was a very difficult time for us both, and we received a lot of criticism. People came and suggested that we wait or even that we shouldn't marry at all. But Simon had peace before God, and although I didn't understand much about the Christian life back then, I trusted him.

One of my friends suggested it would be better if we lived together but didn't get married. I wouldn't have done that before I became a Christian, and I certainly wouldn't have at this point. I think she thought my becoming a Christian was a phase I would grow out of... hopefully before I got around to marrying Simon! Some of my friends even fell out with me for marrying him.

My father gave me away on the day and my mother helped to look after the children, who were page boys. Only four of my six siblings came to the wedding, and none of Nigel's family attended. I totally understood this, as it would have been incredibly hard for them to see their daughter-in-law or sister-in-law remarry at the church where the funeral of their beloved son or brother had taken place. They very kindly sent us a card and gift.

Marrying Simon was one of the hardest things I have ever done. Not only was I doing something that many people were concerned about, or even dead set against, but there were also financial implications. As soon as I walked down the aisle and said yes, I would lose my widow's pension, and if our marriage failed, he would have been entitled to half of everything I owned. Had that happened, I wouldn't have been able to keep my house and would have had to get a job while the boys were still young. It just didn't bear thinking about.

It wasn't easy for Simon, either, as he also had to make sacrifices. He had to give up his push bike and start driving my new car! Seriously, though…

Having been accepted for Baptist ministry training, Spurgeon's College asked Simon to put his calling on hold and learn how to be a husband and father first. This turned out to be such godly wisdom, but it was a disappointment to him at the time. In the years that followed, we felt we were clearly being redirected away from training for ministry in the Baptist Church to the Elim Pentecostal Church. Being part of the Elim family has been a wonderful blessing to us as a couple and as a family.

A new marriage is challenging for everyone

Remarrying will always be a challenge for the relatives of the person who has died. Not only are they working through their grief and emotions, but they are also having to get used to life without their loved one, knowing that someone else might take their place at some point. That's not easy. In fact, it's really tough. Things can never be the same again.

However, widows and widowers also find themselves in a vortex of grief, loss and loneliness. Expecting them to remain single for the rest of their days is a massive ask. I believe we were all created by God to be in relationship; primarily with him, but also with others. We all need love, support and companionship. It is my suggestion that when someone is bereaved, lots of love, patience and understanding is needed from everyone around them.

I'm sure Simon and I didn't get everything right at the time, but I'm happy to say that we still have a wonderful relationship with all those who knew us and remain close to Nigel's family. They are very special to us.

Becoming a family

After getting married in 1987, we continued to live in the house Nigel and I had lived in, but after a couple of years we felt the need to move on and purchase a new home that we could make our own. We also moved churches so we could make a completely fresh start and be known as a family unit.

Our daughter Sarah was born shortly after we moved into our new home in Mountsorrel. We were overjoyed to have a daughter and the boys loved their little sister. She became a much-loved addition to the wider family.

Still learning how to be a husband and father to three young boys, Simon was working as a newsagent, a job he thoroughly enjoyed. Then in January 1992 we both felt directed by God that it was time for Simon to train for ministry, so in September 1992 we relocated to Nantwich in Cheshire to train for pastoral ministry at Elim Bible College.

In February 1994, while we were still training, our second daughter Amy was born. We were overjoyed by Amy's arrival and she made our family complete, but I was still struggling with a number of issues. With unresolved grief and anger to contend with, and a constant feeling of failure following me around, God really had his work cut out with me! But thankfully he is a miracle-working God, as you'll see in Part Two. And he can do the same for you.

Like a wave

Sometimes the wave is small,
You can see it coming from afar
You can feel it as it emerges
And so you brace yourself
Wait for it to break
And let it wash over you.
It's momentary, its over
And you're still standing.

But sometimes that wave is much bigger.
It's dark and deep,
All-consuming and unstoppable.
It arrives suddenly and unexpectantly
And you don't feel it coming until it's too late,
Until it's right there beside you,
towering above you.
Bearing down on you,
Ready to break.
And so you fear it.

You know you only have
moments before it catches
you and comes crashing down.
You wonder if you are going to make it
And so you start walking,

You run,
Until you are submerged and
all you can do is swim
And keep on swimming,
until it's over and you can
breathe again,
You have to ride it out
Because if you don't you'll
drown.

Sara Ward[7]

Chapter 6

Understanding my grief

"The reality is that you will grieve forever. You will not 'get over'
the loss of a loved one; you will learn to live with it. You will heal,
and you will rebuild yourself around the loss you have suffered.
You will be whole again, but you will never be the same.
Nor should you be the same, nor would you want to."
(Elisabeth Kübler-Ross and David Kessler)[8]

According to the Kübler-Ross model there are five stages of grief: shock, denial, anger, depression and acceptance.[9] I discovered that I had to go through all of these stages; I couldn't just skip one. I once heard a lady say that you can't outrun grief, as it will find you wherever you go. She was right. I also had to face up to some of my own issues before I was able to walk in the freedom God had created me for as one of his children.

I had a friend who never grieved for her beloved grandma. Sadly, she had a breakdown more than twenty years later because she had buried it and never faced up to her feelings. One day it rose to the surface because her mind and body simply couldn't cope with keeping it inside any more. She ended up on a psychiatric ward for months.

I'm not suggesting this will happen to everyone, but it highlights the importance of grieving properly. It is a natural process that God designed to allow our minds and bodies to heal and be fully restored following the loss of a loved one.

However, we don't all go through the various stages at the same time or react in the same way. Recognising this, we must be patient, particularly with close family members, allowing each other time and space to grieve. We must remember that not only are they hurting too, but that they are almost certainly going through a different stage from us.

One day at a time

Tris, the protagonist in Veronica Roth's novel, *Insurgent*, says: "Grief is not as heavy as guilt, but it takes more away from you."[10] This was my experience. Grief is exhausting, as it releases all sorts of feelings and emotions. It's possible to feel abandoned, alone, anxious, bereft, confused, heartbroken, lost, lonely, bitter (why me?) and miserable, to name just a few. Some days I felt totally depressed and wondered what the point of life was. My head was all over the place and I felt as though I was drowning. I had to learn to take each day as it came, focusing on one day at a time.

Grief hits when you least expect it

In time, I discovered that it was possible to go days, weeks, months or even years without grief and emotions overwhelming me, and then suddenly a memory or special event would trigger that grief response. This still happens, and when it does it can paralyse me, and the grief can feel overwhelming.

In Malcolm Duncan's book *Good Grief,* he likens grief to the sea: "It can appear calm and still one moment and be whipped up into a violent and threatening storm the next."[11] That really sums up my experience on this journey. In the next few chapters I will share my experiences of these emotions and additional areas in which I really struggled. Thankfully, God had a plan to restore and rebuild my life...

Chapter 7

Overcoming anger

"'In your anger do not sin': Do not let the sun go down while you are still angry." (Ephesians 4:26)

I experienced so much anger after Nigel's death. I had grown up with six siblings, and we had often had fights and disagreements – I even remember losing my temper sometimes – but it was nothing like this. This anger came from deep within me, and it was like an explosion erupting from nowhere.

A few days after the funeral I remember rushing down to the cemetery and shouting at Nigel's grave. I was so angry with him. *How dare you die and leave me?* I demanded. *I can't look after the children and run our home on my own! I need you more now than I ever have before!* Nigel had always done so much for me, and I had no idea how I was going to cope without him. I remember kneeling on the ground, hitting his grave and screaming at him.

The emotional pain of losing someone close will almost always result in an outpouring of anger like the one I have just described. As well as the obvious effects, it can lead to or exacerbate health issues such as headaches, digestive problems, abdominal pains, anxiety, high blood pressure, depression, insomnia, skin problems such as eczema and, in extreme cases, heart attacks and strokes. This is why we need to deal with it as soon as possible.

The anger didn't suddenly disappear when I married Simon. If anything, it actually became worse. I would lose my temper over the stupidest things and then sulk for days on end. I was so angry with everyone and everything! I didn't think it was fair that I had to go through so much just to be part of a happy family.

When I took the children out, I would see other families with their dads and the anger would start rising up inside me because I knew we would never be able to experience that again. I remember sitting in McDonald's with the boys one day, watching a family on the next table laughing and joking. I was so upset. The pain was so real I felt it on a physical level. My chest became tight with anxiety, my head hurt, and I became physically exhausted and emotionally overwhelmed by my feelings.

I knew I needed to get out of there as quickly as possible, but the boys hadn't finished their food. I was hurrying them along, telling them they could take it with them, but we needed to go. The poor little things had no idea how tough I was finding the experience.

No one to talk to

I had so much emotion bottled up in my mind that I was unable to tell people about it. If I had an argument with Simon I couldn't talk to a friend or family member about it, as the majority felt we shouldn't have married in the first place. Many believed our marriage wouldn't last. I felt that if I admitted I was having a tough time, and that we were arguing a lot, they would say, "We told you it wouldn't work." I sensed that one or two people were just waiting for the relationship to fall apart. The only people who supported us one hundred per cent were Simon's relatives, and I obviously couldn't tell them how bad things were either.

I hadn't been a Christian for long, so pouring my heart out to God didn't come naturally to me. I had always sorted my own problems out or talked them over with my family. The first thing I had always done in a crisis was pick up the phone and call a relative or close friend, but I couldn't do that as I felt so isolated from so many of my loved ones.

My anger really affected our marriage and our little family. Sometimes we would go out somewhere, and if Simon said something I didn't like I would be absolutely fuming and allow it to ruin the whole day.

One Christmas I was really angry while we were travelling to stay with my sister Jackie. I was about seven months pregnant with Amy and felt so angry with Simon that I opened the car door, ready to jump out while it was still moving. He managed to grab my arm and forced me to close the door. The children were screaming, and at least one of them remembers it to this day. It hurts me to think that they had to see what I was like back then.

Smashing things and running away

I lost it with Nigel's family not long after Nigel died. I remember going out into the garage and bashing the old car we had with a mallet. I was so cross I just wanted to hurt someone or something. It did help to get rid of some of the aggression I felt, but I don't recommend doing it to those who have decent cars. Ours was just about to be scrapped! It wasn't really his relatives I was cross with, but we often take our anger out on those we are closest to, and because I had spent so much time with them before he passed away, Nigel's siblings were like family to me.

A friend of mine suggested I should go and get a chipped piece of crockery out of the cupboard when I felt angry and throw it against the garden wall to release some of it. That was okay, and it helped for a while, but I soon ran out of chipped mugs and plates and didn't want to start on the decent ones!

Anger makes us do things we would never normally do. One of the incidents Simon often shares relates to a time when I threw his alarm clock down the stairs at him while we were having a massive row and it smashed to bits. I was furious and wanted to hurt him – emotionally rather than physically, though. He was a newsagent at the time and had to get up at four every morning. As it was before the days of mobile phones, he really needed an alarm clock. He was not impressed at all, but we laugh about it now!

Often when we had a row, I found that I just needed to get out of the house, so in a fit of rage I would grab my car keys, slam the door and drive off. Going out for a drive on my own and screaming out loud helped me release some of my feelings. Out of sheer frustration, Simon used to sarcastically sing: "When the going gets tough, Julia gets going." That really didn't help! Another thing that exacerbated the situation was when he used to tell me to "cool it". Never in the history of womankind has a man saying these words resulted in the woman calming down, as Simon repeatedly discovered!

One day I was so angry that I jumped into my car, tore off down the road like a maniac and bought a packet of cigarettes at the local shop. I hadn't smoked for years and knew Simon hated it. I smoked one as I drove home, and as I did so I saw one of our church elders driving towards me. I instantly dropped the cigarette onto the floor of the car and opened the window, desperately trying to get rid of the smoke before he saw me.

I also remember going to visit a lovely couple from the church for a meal. We'd had an awful row before we left the house and I hadn't spoken to Simon all the way there. While we were at the couple's house I acted normally, so Simon thought I was fine, but as soon as we left I ignored him again. Bless him, he tried so hard with me and was incredibly patient. My anger overwhelmed me at times, and I must have been far from easy to live with.

The new spouse in any existing family also faces many challenges. It is never easy as they navigate a new relationship, particularly if there are children involved. Simon wasn't Nigel, but sometimes I expected him to respond or behave as Nigel would have done and became frustrated and angry if he didn't. I had to learn to be patient and to make allowances, just as he had to with me. That's what makes a good marriage work.

Set free

A few years later I went to a conference in London and heard American pastor and author Lisa Bevere share her testimony of how God had set her free from anger. I had thought I was the world's worst in the anger stakes until I heard her story, but boy had she been angry! I realised that if God could set her free from that intense kind of anger he could definitely sort me out.

Lisa said that if anyone wanted God to set them free from anger, they should stand up right where they were. I stood with scores of other women and she prayed for us. To be honest, I never really thought any more about it until about three months later when I suddenly realised God had set me free. I no longer felt angry with everyone all the time.

I won't say that I have never become angry since, as I'm still human. However, I am more aware that I need to manage my emotions more effectively, and if I feel any anger rising, I simply pray about the situation and give it to God. I never want to experience that constant feeling of rage again. We all feel anger at times, but it should never become a constant state. It's what we do with our anger that can tip us over into wrongdoing and rob us of our peace.

What the Bible says about anger

> *"'In your anger do not sin.' Do not let the sun go down while you are still angry, and do not give the devil a foothold"* (Ephesians 4:26-27).

Simon quoted this verse to me regularly because I often went to bed fuming with him, so I came to know it really well! He always tried so hard to put things right before bed, but I was having none of it. He would eventually give up and go to sleep, which made me even angrier!

How can he sleep when I'm so upset? I would wonder. *Doesn't he care about me and how I'm feeling?* He couldn't win! I would lie there for hours and hours, tossing and turning, unable to sleep because I was so cross. I would relive all our arguments in my mind and blame him for absolutely everything. Then I would feel really ill in the morning, as I was exhausted, and then I would be grumpier than ever.

Looking back, it's clear that my immediate anger at whatever I felt Simon had done, quickly developed into something way out of proportion. I allowed that initial angry response to expand to the point where it included everything I was unhappy with or had previously been angry about. In fact, my anger caused me to lose many a night's sleep. It wasn't good for our marriage or for our children. My problem was that I had been keeping a record of all Simon's wrongs and needed to learn to forgive him more frequently, so my anger didn't build up.

I'm always challenged by these words the apostle Paul declared:

"...[Love] keeps no record of wrongs" (1 Corinthians 13:5).

What a challenge for each one of us. Paul states that we must not sin in our anger. The fact that he highlights this suggests anger is a common problem. It is a tool the enemy uses, and, as we all know, it can soon escalate out of control. We must guard against this in all our relationships, and even more so in our closest relationships. The Bible encourages us to make allowances for each other's faults, to show grace, mercy and love, and to forgive anyone who offends us.

"Therefore, as God's chosen people, holy and dearly loved, clothe yourselves with compassion, kindness, humility, gentleness and patience. Bear with each other and forgive one another if any of you has a grievance against someone. Forgive as the Lord forgave you. And over all these virtues put on love, which binds them all together in perfect unity. Let the peace of Christ rule in your hearts, since as members of one body you were called to peace. And be thankful" (Colossians 3:12-15).

Get rid!

Paul also encouraged the Colossian believers to get rid of numerous negative attitudes and behaviours (see Colossians 3:8). Top of the list? You guessed it: anger! Perhaps you've noticed that people have generally become angrier over the past few years. We must guard against this, asking God to help us rid our hearts and lives of the scourge of anger.

"…Remember, the Lord forgave you, so you must forgive others" (Colossians 3:13, NLT).

Another passage that helped me is James 1:19-20:

"My dear brothers and sisters, take note of this: Everyone should be quick to listen, slow to speak and slow to become angry, because human anger does not produce the righteousness that God desires."

God wants us to listen to others and take time to think about what we say in response. Once a word is out of our mouths we cannot take it back. I can guarantee you that the negative words will be the ones the other person remembers for a long time, maybe even forever. Words can be so hurtful, and they have the potential to do so much damage.

I used to say exactly what I thought in an argument. I just wanted to hurt the person I was arguing with. My reasoning was that I was hurting, so why shouldn't they be? I'm sure you will have heard the saying that "hurt people hurt people", and they do. I can testify to that.

Sorry seems to be the hardest word

Another thing I really struggled with was saying sorry. It wasn't something that was said very much while I was growing up. As a family we would fall out for a while, then eventually it would fade away and life would carry on as normal. No one ever appeared to say sorry or attempted to forgive and make up.

I honestly never thought I needed to say sorry, as it wasn't ever my fault! I know how wrong that was now. Poor Simon!

He really went through the mill with me. To this day I am amazed he stuck with me, as I made his life such a misery during those early years of marriage. He never knew what I was going to be like from one day to the next. I thank God for him and for the firm Christian foundations his parents built into his life. Simon recently told me that when I was becoming difficult to live with, he regularly prayed, "Lord, do something with her!" Praise God that he did.

I have discovered that it's important to say sorry to people, sometimes even when we don't feel we have done anything particularly wrong. An apology always opens the door to reconciliation and healing, and this is really important for our relationships with others and with God. He expects us to be reconciled with one another and to be at peace in all our relationships.

> *"Therefore, if you are offering your gift at the altar and there remember that your brother or sister has something against you, leave your gift there in front of the altar. First go and be reconciled to them; then come and offer your gift"* (Matthew 5:23-24).

Time to allow God in?

If anything in this chapter resonates with how you are feeling, my heart's desire is that you will allow God to minister to you. Please don't just accept that this is the way you are. Consider the fact that God wants you to be completely free so you can live an abundant and fulfilling life that is not hamstrung by your past or present behaviour in any way.

I know people who have found Christ and been set free of something straight away, so don't think that you can't be set free if you have only just committed to a relationship with him, because anything is possible with God. He can move the issues that feel like mountains in our lives.

> *"'Truly I tell you, if anyone says to this mountain, "Go throw yourself into the sea," and does not doubt in their heart, but believes that what they say will happen, it will be done for them'"* (Mark 11:23).

It's OK to feel angry, particularly if you have lost a loved one. This is a natural human response to a huge loss, and God understands our anger. It needs to be released somehow, just not towards others. Throwing a few old cups against a wall or going for a walk in the countryside and having a good scream can really help.

We can also talk to our Father in heaven, who willingly sacrificed His one and only Son on the cross and understands our pain and sense of loss. We can tell him exactly how we feel. Lay it all out before Him. It doesn't matter how long that takes; God will listen. When you have finished, ask him to take that anger away and set you free from it. Ask him to fill you with his peace, which surpasses all understanding (see Philippians 4:7).

I would also encourage you to write down everything you have talked to God about in a journal. Then, whenever you are struggling, you can go back and see what God has done for you.

Prayer

Here's a prayer that might help. Please feel free to adapt it, using your own words:

"Father, help me in my sadness and loss. My heart aches for [name your lost loved one]. I'm struggling to understand and take in what has happened.

Why me? Why now? Why? I feel so numb and I miss him/her so much. I have no idea how I can carry on.

I'm feeling so angry with you, with him/her and with others right now. Nobody understands my pain, my anguish, my despair or my anger. But I don't want to feel angry any more, Father. I hate feeling angry.

Please forgive me for allowing anger to become a foothold. I refuse to be influenced by it for a second longer, and I ask you to set me free from it in Jesus' name. I forgive those I need to forgive and pray that you will replace my anger with your incredible peace, which surpasses all understanding. May it completely fill my heart and mind in Christ Jesus. Amen."

Don't rush away from this prayer. Allow that incredible peace of God to flow into you and envelope you completely. Allow him to minister deeply into your spirit through his Holy Spirit.

Chapter 8

Facing my fears

*"Being brave isn't the absence of fear.
Being brave is having that fear but
finding a way through it."* (Bear Grylls)[12]

Thanatophobia – a fear of losing someone you love – is very common. The word comes from the Greek words "thanato", which means death, and "phobia", which means fear. Symptoms of thanatophobia include distress, anxiety and dread.

When the worst thing that could ever happen to you happens, it will undoubtedly create fear. It's a fact that bad stuff happens to good people. After Nigel died I was left with an overwhelming fear of dying, or of my children dying. I would find myself dreaming that one of them had died and wake up in a cold sweat. Then I would rush into their bedrooms to check they were still breathing.

Fearing the worst

When Simon and I got married, I believed with all my heart that he was going to die. If he was ever late home I would convince myself that he must be dead. I would draw all the curtains, sit in darkness at the bottom of the stairs and start planning his funeral in my mind. *Where is he?* I would wonder. *Is he dead in a ditch somewhere?* The worst possible thoughts would race through my mind. I even thought about the people I wouldn't invite to his funeral because they hadn't wanted us to get married in the first place! I decided I wouldn't let anyone enter the house this time, as I couldn't go through all that again. The longer I waited for him, the angrier and more fearful I became.

By the time Simon eventually came home I would be fuming, and I usually worked myself up into such a state that I would shout and scream at him. I feel so sorry for our poor neighbours! *Why can't you just let me know you're running late?* I would demand. This was in the days before mobile phones, so it wasn't always possible to do so, but I was so anxious and fearful because I firmly believed that history was going to repeat itself.

As I lay next to Simon at night, I would hear his heart beating and suddenly be taken back to listening to Nigel's. Nigel's heart condition had caused his heart to beat too slowly, so sometimes I had lain there counting how many beats there were a minute. I started wondering whether I should count Simon's beats per minute. *What if it's slower than it should be… or faster?* I also listened to him breathing while he was asleep. If I couldn't hear anything, I would nudge him in the hope that he would move so I knew he was still alive.

Then I would start to think to myself, *What if I wake up in the morning and he's died in the night?* That had happened to a lady I worked with not long before I remarried, so this fear was plausible, and it began to consume and control me. I later realised it was because I couldn't believe that I would ever be happy again, and that if I were, something would inevitably come along and spoil it.

After Sarah was born, I had the most horrific recurring nightmare that I had found her dead in her cot. It became so real that I couldn't sleep at night because I was so worried about her. If the thought entered my mind that I should check on her I would have to do so straight away, as I had convinced myself that if she died it would be my fault and I would never forgive myself. I would be up and down all night, checking on her. It was exhausting, and the more tired I became the more anxious I felt. In the end, it became a vicious circle.

I received prayer for my thanatophobia, but I hadn't been a Christian very long, so giving things to God wasn't something I knew how to do. For thirty years of my life I had made my own decisions, worried about everything myself and just lived life the way I wanted. Suddenly having to grasp how to live as a Christian alongside the grief and loss I was experiencing was quite a challenge! I began to wonder if I was actually a Christian, as my life was such a struggle.

Fear can engulf us to the point that we are unable to think rationally. We can become so afraid that we don't even want to get up in the morning because we're scared of what the day might bring. If you are experiencing thanatophobia or any other sort of fear, try to share your feelings with those closest to you, get some professional help and create healthy coping mechanisms to help you manage the fear.

Had Nigel gone to heaven?

One of the things I became really fearful about was whether Nigel had invited Jesus into his heart before he died and whether he had gone to heaven or not. Whenever there was an appeal for salvation at our family services, I would start to wonder how I could know either way. I remembered my mum saying that Nigel would never have become a Christian because he wasn't like that. I'm not sure what she thought a person had to be like in order to become a Christian.

Years after he died, I was sitting in a family service, thinking about this as the appeal was made, when God spoke to me as clearly as anything. He said, "What did Stuart Clarke pray on the day Nigel died?" Stuart's words returned to me like a flash of light: "If it's your will that he should be with you in paradise today, we give you permission to take him." It was at that moment that Nigel had passed peacefully away. I finally knew, once and for all, that Nigel was in heaven and that I would see him again one day.

Addressing my fears

A few weeks after relocating to Birmingham to take up a new ministry role in 2019, I had the most awful nightmare. I had never experienced such a bad dream since the recurring ones about Sarah. I dreamed that someone had broken into our house and attacked me and Simon in our beds, and it had felt so real that I was shaking all over. I literally screamed, jumped out of bed and ran across the room! Simon calmed me down and talked to me about other things, as I was petrified of going back to sleep. The next night I was so scared it would happen again that I didn't want to go to bed at all.

I felt this way for about a week, until eventually I forgot about it. It helped that we had prayed every night that God would take the thoughts away. Since then I have had another couple of nightmares along the same lines, but when it happens now I try to put it into perspective, reassuring myself that whatever I am afraid of is actually very unlikely to come to pass. Regardless of our circumstances, it is always helpful to rationalise the situation rather than dwelling on our fears about what could happen.

It's easy to see how the enemy uses fear to impact many areas of our lives. We simply mustn't allow this. We need to make a choice not to allow fear to control our lives and ask God to help us overcome our fears.

Fear does not come from God, so we should look at what he says about it in the Bible and start living it out. He doesn't want us to live in fear of what might happen. Our fears can appear very real to us, and probably even more so the more we dwell upon them. It is far better to dwell on God's promises than fears that could potentially overwhelm us.

One day I was having a conversation with God out loud as I drove to fetch our youngest daughter, Amy, from nursery. This was the only time I seemed to be on my own most weeks. I was telling him I wasn't ready to die, and that I didn't want Simon or the children to die either, when I felt him remind me of a verse:

> *"For I know the plans I have for you,' declares the Lord, 'plans to prosper you and not to harm you, plans to give you hope and a future'"* (Jeremiah 29:11).

It was as if a light had been switched on. God revealed that he had plans for me, so I knew I wasn't going to die until they had been fulfilled. He wasn't going to allow any harm to come to me, and I felt assured that Simon and the children were going to be all right. He actually had a great future planned for me! Even though I knew that verse off by heart by this point, I had never seen it like that before.

Amy's fear

We used to say that Amy was frightened of her own shadow. She was scared of being left in the house on her own and of going into the garage at night. She has always been terrified of mice, and we had quite a few in our garage in Newcastle at times!

I recently heard her share her testimony at the City Women conference at City Gates Church in Ilford, London, where her husband Ore is youth pastor. I was aware that she was fearful, but I never realised how much it had impacted her life until that day.

While she was sharing her testimony, she was asked the following question: "Something happened to you that changed things for you. What was it?"

She replied that her best friend, Sarah, had died unexpectedly in her sleep in 2014. Amy had been one of the first people to hear about Sarah's death. The two girls had been having a text conversation the night before and Sarah had suddenly stopped replying, so she rang the house phone the following day to find out where she was, only to be told by Sarah's father that he had just discovered her body.

Amy said that although this was a very tragic and devastating time for her, the long-term loss of Sarah had a positive impact on her relationship with Jesus. Initially, though, it had made her very fearful. Sometimes if she didn't hear from someone for a while, she was afraid something terrible must have happened to them. This affected her so badly that she became scared to return home from university and open the front door in case she found me or Simon dead at the bottom of the stairs. She acknowledged that fear had crept into every area of her life and heavily impacted the way she lived.

The next question she was asked was: "How and when did you become aware that fear was taking over your life?"

She said that around two years after Sarah died, she had been helping Ore lock the fire exits at the Dream Centre in Newcastle (where Simon and I were senior pastors) after an evening meeting. The building is massive and has about eleven exits, some of which are down in the basement, so they are quite dark and isolated. Even though the building was secure and alarmed, Amy was petrified that someone might be hiding somewhere, waiting to kill her. Ore told her this fear issue was getting pretty ridiculous and that it had too much of a hold over her life.

It had come to a point where she had to deal with it. Ore helped her see that she couldn't go on living like this, and that it wasn't what God wanted for her (or any of us). He drew her attention to this verse:

"For God has not given us a spirit of fear, but of power and of love and of a sound mind" (2 Timothy 1:7, NKJV).

She started repeating this scripture aloud, over and over again; praying through the verse and standing on it. There is such power in declaring the truth of God's Word over your life. She had to play her part in this and start walking in the knowledge that there is nothing to be fearful of if we trust that God has a hope and a future for us. She spent time with God, giving the fear to him, and although it didn't go away immediately, her life began to change for the better.

The impact of fear

I've described the way fear impacted me as a young widow, wife and mother, but there are countless other ways it can destroy our lives. The enemy comes to steal, kill and destroy (see John 10:10) and will use fear to rob us of our confidence, courage, joy, peace, contentment, creativity and all the rewards of faith. If allowed to do so, he will immobilise us, limiting and controlling us to the point where we are unwilling to take any risks or step out in faith, which causes us to miss out on being all that God has called us to be.

I wonder what you are fearful of. It may not be dying or losing someone close, but you may fear getting cancer or becoming seriously ill. Maybe you're afraid of flying, spiders, the dark, unemployment, failure (I'll talk more about this later), embarrassment, rejection, commitment, old age or being alone. You might even be fearful of a person: a partner, boss, work colleague, friend, family member or neighbour.

We may start to believe the lie that God can never forgive or love us, or that we will never be happy or that our lives are pointless. We may fear that we will never be able to do the things we would like to do, or that we will never meet that life partner and have a family. We may fear that we can't break a habit or addiction we have been struggling with, or that the past will hold us back forever.

Like anger, fear doesn't just affect us spiritually; it can also affect us physically. It can lead to ulcers, irritable bowel syndrome (IBS), allergies, tremors, decreased fertility and cardiovascular damage as well as weakening our immune systems. This gives us even more reason to deal with the fear in our lives so we can feel better physically and spiritually, and so we can step into the life God has for us.

God doesn't want us to be controlled by fear. He wants us to live life to the full, at peace with everyone and everything. That is the life he has called us to. Fear can stop us doing so many of the amazing things he has planned for us. It can stop us taking that step of faith into a new ministry opportunity, applying for that promotion at work, saying yes to that new relationship or moving to that new city or country. It robs us of so many of the good things he has for each one of us. God has a plan for our lives. It may be difficult at times, but he is there with us every step of the way and will bring us through it. Best of all, we will be so much stronger for it.

He is not a God of fear, but a God of love:

"There is no fear in love. But perfect love drives out fear, because fear has to do with punishment. The one who fears is not made perfect in love" (1 John 4:18).

His desire is that we live without fear, and his perfect love is more than capable of destroying it. Why do you think God put "fear not" in the Bible 365 times? I think he knew that in the natural we would be fearful people, so he provided a "fear not" for every day of the year!

God encouraged Joshua not to be fearful as he took up the leadership of the children of Israel from Moses and commenced the conquest of the Promised Land: the land flowing with milk and honey. He said this several times:

"Have I not commanded you? Be strong and courageous. Do not be afraid; do not be discouraged, for the Lord your God will be with you wherever you go" (Joshua 1:9).

When God commands something it is always for our own good. He has promised that he will be with us and that we are not on our own, so there is no need for us to be afraid. He later said to the Israelites:

"So do not fear, for I am with you; do not be dismayed, for I am your God. I will strengthen you and help you; I will uphold you with my righteous right hand" (Isaiah 41:10).

We can spend so much time and energy worrying about the things we're afraid of, when in reality the majority will never happen. I often listen to a song that talks about us not being slaves to fear because we are the children of God. This really helps me to stop feeling fearful about life's challenges.

Mastering our fear

Fear will always be part of the fallen world we live in and will, on occasion, come knocking on our doors. There will be times in our lives when we naturally become anxious and fearful, but we need to learn how to master it rather than allowing it to master us. Like Amy, we may need to work at this over time.

If you are struggling, ask God to help you overcome your fears. Take a look at the Bible and see what he says about fear. Meditate on those scriptures, write them down and put them somewhere prominent, where you will see them each time you walk past. Declare them out loud each day until you no longer feel fearful. You could use the verse above from 2 Timothy 1:7 as a starting point. Declare it out loud and name your fear before God. Refuse to submit to it.

If you feel you need further support, talk to a friend or pastor and ask for prayer. Sharing with a friend often helps us see things more clearly.

Remember this: you are deeply loved and cherished by God. He knows absolutely everything about you; more than you know yourself! He was there at the beginning of our lives and will be there when we take our final breaths... and everywhere in-between. Even in the times when we don't sense his presence, he is with us. Whatever you have experienced, and whatever you might face in the future, do not fear. As the following verse shows, the God who really knows you will continue to protect, provide for and sustain you:

> *"Are not five sparrows sold for two copper coins? And not one of them is forgotten before God. But the very hairs on your head are all numbered. Do not fear therefore; you are of more value than many sparrows"* (Luke 12:6-7, NKJV).

Prayer

"Thank you, Father, that you have not given me a spirit of fear, but a spirit of power, love and a sound mind. I recognise that my world has become quite a fearful place, so I choose to let go of every fear I have today [list them before God] and give them to you. I refuse to be a slave to fear any longer, because I am your child.

I choose faith over fear and peace over anxiety. Help me to recognise when I am becoming fearful in the future and to choose not dwell in that place but rather to fix my eyes on you, the one who said: 'So do not fear, for I am with you; do not be dismayed, for I am your God. I will strengthen you and help you; I will uphold you with my righteous right hand.' Amen."

You might want to pray this prayer every day until you realise that fear is no longer an issue for you.

Chapter 9

Guilt-free living

"Therefore, there is now no condemnation for those who are in Christ Jesus." (Romans 8:1)

Guilt also played a massive part in my life after Nigel's death. I felt guilty about absolutely everything I did or even thought about. I also became highly sensitive to how other people felt about the way I lived my life. I desperately wanted everyone to be happy. I always believed it was my fault if someone was upset with me.

Sometimes I felt it was my fault that Nigel had died so young. *He enjoyed a good old English fry-up, but perhaps I shouldn't have let him have one every week*, I would think to myself. *All that fat couldn't have been good for him. Also, he moved furniture into the new house; he even carried a fridge on his own! I should never have allowed him to do anything like that.* Thoughts like these continually flooded my mind and made me feel dreadful.

I felt I should have done so many things differently after Nigel died and felt particularly guilty for bringing extra worry and upset to my parents' door. They had done so much for me, and I felt I had let them down. All I had ever wanted was to make them proud of me,

I felt guilty if I left the children with anyone, if I disciplined them, if I went out with friends or treated myself. I was wracked with guilt about everything: being alive when Nigel was dead, having him cremated rather than buried, snapping at him the week before he died. Anything I could think of, I felt guilty about. It had taken over my whole life and become quite overwhelming.

Money matters

Nigel and I had never really had much money. We had a big mortgage and were always struggling to keep on top of things financially. When he died, I was given a pension and a young widow's mother's allowance. It wasn't a proper state widow's pension, as I was too young to be classed as a widow. You had to be over forty, which really annoyed me at the time. How can there be an age limit? Either you're a widow or you aren't!

All of a sudden I had more money than we had ever had as a couple. I felt so guilty about this. It didn't seem right that Nigel had needed to die in order for me and the boys to live more comfortably. The only thing that made me feel better at that time was shopping, but then I felt even guiltier for spending money I had never had before when I got home. I'm so glad there wasn't any online shopping back then, or goodness knows what I would have bought and how much I would have spent. It doesn't bear thinking about!

Nigel had taken out a life insurance policy to make sure the boys and I would be okay while they were little if anything happened to him. We had owned an old wreck of a car, and after his death my dad suggested that I should get a new one. I needed a reliable, safe vehicle to take the children out in. My uncle managed to get me a really good deal on a brand new Ford Escort Ghia. I think the salesmen felt sorry for the young widow with her three little boys.

The boys and I loved the car, especially as it had a CD player, which was a real treat back in the day. We played Wham! everywhere we went; so much so that we knew most of the words off by heart.

Nigel's father, Roland, told me I was being criticised at the village pub for spending Nigel's money on a new car. *Hello!* I thought to myself. *It isn't Nigel's money. He's dead, so he can't spend it!* In fairness, Roland stuck up for me and told them it was none of their business.

Finding love again

The deepest guilt that settled on and stayed with me for a long while was meeting Simon. *How can I possibly feel something for another man when my husband had just died?* My heart ached for Nigel and I couldn't really understand what was happening to me.

I later realised that a lot of my guilt was caused by other people. Their lack of understanding of everything I was experiencing, and their inability to realise that at some point a widow or widower might well fall in love again, and that this is normal, made me feel so guilty. There is no rule book on timing, either.

When Simon and I got engaged, a single lady from the church he had known for years found out and said that it wasn't fair. I had already been married once and she never had. I felt so bad about it and was genuinely upset.

Then we discovered that certain friends wouldn't come to our wedding because they didn't approve of the marriage. Several of my relatives fell out with me and some didn't speak to me for years. Someone really close to me said it was unforgivable for me to even see anyone, let alone marry him. I haven't had a proper conversation with that friend since that day; not because I haven't forgiven him, but because I suspect he is still struggling to come to terms with it because he hasn't forgiven me.

I recognise that this whole period was difficult for everyone, and I'm sure I wasn't the easiest person to live with at times, as my emotions were all over the place, but all of these conversations and incidents compounded my guilt. Sadly, people don't always realise how damaging their comments are to someone who is already coming to terms with the worst loss they will probably ever face.

Honeymoon guilt

I remember sitting at Heathrow Airport the day after our wedding, waiting to fly to Greece for our honeymoon. Simon had gone to check the flight times, and as I waited for him to return I experienced an overwhelming sense of guilt. *What have I done? Are my friends and family members right? Have I done the right thing?*

Simon knew something was wrong when he returned, as I was a bit off with him. The problem was, I felt guilty for getting married and going away on honeymoon, and then I also felt guilty for feeling guilty about it. I should have been happy that I had been given the opportunity to marry again and for the boys to have a father. It wasn't until years later that I told Simon what had been going on in my mind.

Guilt does not come from God

As I look back now, I can see that guilt had become a massive issue for me, but with God's help I managed to identify and work through it. If you have invited Jesus into your life, God will never condemn you for any sin or shame you feel. It is not his plan that we should live in a state of guilt.

The enemy uses guilt to entrap us. He wants us to be so riddled with this feeling that it affects all areas of our lives. But we will never move forward and experience all that he has for us if we are constantly living in guilt. We have to choose which voice we will listen to: Jesus' or the enemy's. Questioning yourself over the things you feel guilty about may help you think more rationally.

Questions I asked myself:

Q: Is it really my fault that Nigel died?

A: No. he had a life-threatening virus that I could not have caused.

Q: Why do I feel guilty about leaving my boys with family members?

A: I did it before Nigel died and it wasn't a problem then. They love going to visit relatives and it's good for them to have some normality in their lives.

Q: Why do I feel guilty about having more money than I did before Nigel died?

A: That was what we had both planned for if something happened to either of us. We wanted to make sure we could provide for the boys as they were growing up, whatever happened.

Q: Why do I feel guilty for loving Simon and wanting to marry him?

A: I hadn't stopped loving Nigel because I had fallen in love with Simon. Nigel would have wanted me and the boys to be happy.

Simon loved me and the boys, and he worked incredibly hard to be the best husband and father he could be. I am convinced that my boys would not be the men they are today if I had brought them up alone.

Q: Why do I feel guilty for disciplining the boys?

A: Nigel was a firm believer that children should be taught to behave themselves and have good manners, and I shared this belief. That's why they were so good most of the time, as they knew their boundaries. A family member suggested I shouldn't tell them off because they had lost their daddy, but I felt I needed more boundaries in place than ever so I could bring up three boys as a single mum. I'm so glad I didn't listen to others on this subject, as I'm not sure Simon would ever have asked me out if I had let them run wild!

Don't allow guilt to take over

If we allow it, guilt will occupy too much of our head space. Struggling to overcome feelings of chronic guilt can have a really bad effect on our health. It can lead to depression, anxiety and other mental health issues. I suffered with depression at times due to the intense guilt I felt.

I have heard various friends make comments about people remarrying after their partners have died over the years, not realising Simon and I married quite quickly after Nigel's death. They can't understand the person wanting to remarry, particularly if it is soon after their loved one's death. They would say how dreadful it was and how they couldn't possibly have done that. Even now I can begin to go down that guilt route as I stand there listening, and I sometimes feel as if I have to defend myself. Then I'm reminded that I don't have to justify myself. I know that marrying Simon when I did was right. God's timing was perfect. It wasn't an easy journey, but I know it was the right one for us and for my little boys, who had no daddy.

I don't feel angry with people for having strong opinions about how long people should wait to get married again or whether people should marry someone younger than themselves. Before I lost Nigel I had many of the same thoughts. I simply didn't understand what it would be like to be in that position. We all have different opinions on many issues, and I like to think that one of the things I learned from this is that we have no idea what people are going through and we need to pray rather than judge.

"Do not judge others, and you will not be judged. For you will be treated as you treat others. The standard you use in judging is the standard by which you will be judged" (Matthew 7:1-2, NLT).

Dealing with guilt and shame

Feelings of guilt and shame can remain with us forever, so we have to learn to deal with them or we will be unable to move forward in the freedom God has given us. We can't afford to keep carrying guilt around with us. We have all made mistakes and have perhaps done things we feel guilty about, but I would encourage anyone who is feeling this way to let go and let God take control. You may need to say sorry to someone in order to break the impasse, even if you feel it wasn't your fault. It's hard to do this, but sometimes we need to be the bigger person.

If there are things in your life that you feel guilty about, I would also encourage you to grab a piece of paper and a pen, and write them down. Then start asking yourself similar questions to the ones I listed earlier. Allow God to help you see the truth and then walk in this new revelation of the truth.

> *"Let us draw near to God with a sincere heart and with the full assurance that faith brings, having our hearts sprinkled to cleanse us from a guilty conscience and having our bodies washed with pure water"* (Hebrews 10:22).

When Jesus died on the cross, he dealt with all our sin, guilt and shame. So draw near to God and ask him to take away any guilt and shame you may be carrying. Then, from this day forward, choose not to listen to the lies and condemnation of the enemy, but rather remember what the Bible says:

> *"Therefore there is now no condemnation [no guilty verdict, no punishment] for those who are in Christ Jesus [who believe in Him as personal Lord and Savior]"* (Romans 8:1, AMP).

Prayer

"Father, thank you for the reminder that there is no guilt or condemnation for those who are in Christ Jesus. I refuse to sit under this guilt and shame for a moment longer. Please forgive me for anything I've done that has contributed to these feelings. I choose to forgive those who have made me feel guilty. Help me experience the peace and presence of your Holy Spirit from now on and to make a choice every day to play to an

audience of one: YOU. May it be my delight to make you smile every day. In Jesus' name. Amen."

Now that you have prayed this prayer, I believe the guilt will be replaced by God's incredible peace.

Romans 5:1 tells us*: "Therefore, since we have been justified by faith, we have peace with God through our Lord Jesus Christ."*

Chapter 10

Facing Failure

"I can do all things through him who gives me strength."
(Philippians 4:13)

As a child I excelled at more or less everything I did, including ballet, swimming, elocution and piano lessons. I absolutely loved junior school and couldn't wait to go each day. I was top of my class every term, and nine times out of ten I got one hundred per cent in my tests. In fact, I really struggled if I got anything less than top marks. I was even allowed to join the year above for algebra lessons as I was so good at maths.

I loved everything about my life until I moved to high school. That's when my life changed for the worse, as I didn't really enjoy it and found the work much more challenging. My junior school had been very small, whereas the private girls' high school was enormous. Many of the girls had been at the school right from kindergarten and had already developed their own friendship groups. I felt different, and that I didn't fit in.

I always blamed myself for ending up there, as I had pleaded with my parents to send me. I was reading a lot of Enid Blyton's *Malory Towers* books at the time, which were based at a girls-only boarding school. I couldn't read the books quickly enough, as the girls always seemed to have so much fun. My best friend was heading off to boarding school and I had begged my parents to let me go with her. I actually had to sit an entrance exam, which I failed, so the school allowed me to do a year at the junior school first and said I would move up to the high school providing that I did well.

I absolutely loathed high school. I missed my family so much that I cried every time I had to return. There were only five boarders in our year; all the rest were day girls. The day girls would come in each day and tell us about all the exciting things they had done or were going to do at the weekends, but we weren't allowed to do anything much apart from hang out in the common room and around the grounds. It was so boring! The only TV we were allowed to watch was *Top of the Pops* every Thursday evening. I was so unhappy.

Every November there was an enormous fair in Loughborough, which meant that all the roads in the centre of town were closed. We were taken to the fair and allowed to separate from the matron for a short time, but we were always in our uniforms. The local children made fun of us, as we stood out like sore thumbs. It was awful.

After a year the school changed to weekly boarders only. This meant we could go home every weekend, so my parents thought I would be a lot happier. I remember my mum saying, "You won't cry when we take you back now, will you?" But as soon as we saw the road sign for Loughborough I would become distressed and start crying. I still hated it, so they decided to move to Rothley, which was closer to the school, and let me attend as a day girl. After five miserable terms, I finally felt more like the rest of the girls in my class.

However, I was bullied by some of the local girls in Rothley during my early teens. They made my life a misery and called me a snob because we lived in a large house on a really nice, tree-lined road just outside the village. I also went to a private school and spoke with a posh accent (which I later spent a long time trying to get rid of, as I wanted to fit in), so that didn't help me much!

They would shout and swear at me when I stood at the bus stop on the opposite side of the road from them, waiting to go to school. I was quite scared at times, especially after I left school and went to college, when I had to stand at the same bus stop as them. They were really horrible to me.

One day they started mocking me and pulling my hair. I couldn't stand it any more. I turned around and gave them a mouthful of expletives that I wouldn't normally have used, but I wanted to use words they would be familiar with. They never said anything to me again. In fact, they ignored me completely until I started seeing Nigel much later, at which point they suddenly changed and started to be nice to me. I can only presume they accepted me because I was going out with a local lad.

I am a failure

I had a major operation on my feet during my teens. I must have missed six weeks of school, and in those days they didn't send any work home. This had a massive impact on my education, and I don't think I ever really caught up. It also knocked my confidence.

I wasn't the best at completing my homework. I used to do it on the bus on the way to school and often copied my friends' work. I remember the whole class getting into trouble once as everyone had copied the same girl's homework and she had made one mistake. It wasn't too hard for the teacher to work out what had happened.

I eventually took my O' levels and found them extremely difficult. I worked hard for them but just couldn't remember much. I was pretty certain I would get a few, which would enable me to return to school for sixth form. I was working for my dad at his knitwear factory on results day and had told my mother to call me as soon as the post came. I got the call and asked how I had got on.

"You didn't pass any of them," she said. Although she never said how she felt about this, I'm sure she was disappointed for me.

"What, not one?" I said. "Not even needlework?" I was surprised because I had excelled in needlework and had been given an A grade for my practical project. "No," she replied.

I put the phone down and ran to the ladies' toilets. I was absolutely distraught and needed to hide myself away somewhere. I sobbed so hard. I couldn't believe I hadn't passed a single one and felt like the end of my life had come. *How is this possible?* I asked myself. *Now what am I going to do?* I cried on and off for three days, and my eyes became so swollen I could hardly open them. From that day on, and for the next thirty years, I felt I was a failure in every area of my life.

We were constantly told by our teachers that O levels were everything, and that without them we might as well give up. I didn't want to go back to school and resit the year because I couldn't face seeing my friends in sixth form. I was so embarrassed and ashamed that I hated seeing anyone because I had to tell them my results. I had always wanted to be a fashion designer – probably because I wanted to please my dad, who was in the industry, and gain his approval – so he called Leicester Polytechnic and enrolled me onto a textile knitwear design course. Don't ask me why I thought I could be a fashion designer, by the way, as my drawing skills were absolutely rubbish!

I completed the two-year course, and to this day I don't know how I passed. I didn't enjoy it at all; in fact, I worked out that I could miss a certain percentage of the course without my parents finding out, so I hardly bothered to attend the lectures I hated most. Seeing I was the only one in my new friendship group with a car, the five of us used to squeeze into my little red Fiat 500 for an afternoon of fun instead of attending lectures.

Years later, I would watch the news where they interviewed young people about their results and I would start to cry. Seeing this brought that painful time back to me as if it were yesterday, and then I felt like even more of a failure.

Then when my children came to take their exams, I was more nervous than they were, and found the whole situation incredibly painful. It brought back so many distressing memories for me. I remember one of Matthew's teachers saying that he seemed incredibly nervous about his junior school exams and she couldn't understand why, as they had purposely played them down. I instantly knew that my fear of failure had affected him and that it was my fault for panicking on his behalf.

The impact of my previous failings was deep and affected so much of my life and my ability to move forward. My confidence was shattered. I would start a new course, new job or even a new role at church and then give it up within days, as I would convince myself I couldn't do it. I always told people there were only two things I could do well: have babies and swim!

I am what I am

I felt like even more of a failure when Simon was called to Elim Bible College in Nantwich, because we were surrounded by students and academics. It brought everything back and I became so miserable and lonely.

Simon introduced me to another student's wife during the first term and she asked what I was planning to study. I said I wasn't going to study as I had four children to take care of. It turned out she already had one degree and was studying for another. When we arrived home I was furious with Simon. I told him not to introduce me to anyone else unless they were thicker than me, which I figured was pretty much impossible. I hated our time there.

It was even worse the following year when we lived on campus. Simon would bring his friends back during coffee breaks and they would talk about their studies. I would dread anyone asking my opinion on anything, as it was all completely over my head.

My failure at school continued to have a massive impact on my life and stopped me being myself. For instance, I never enjoyed going to our church connect groups, which met in people's homes, in case I was put on the spot. When I first started seeing Simon we went to one together, and at the end the leader gave us some homework to do. I did mine, but the day before the next meeting I did it again with Simon and copied all his answers because I was convinced mine would be wrong. When we got to the group, I discovered that my answers had all been correct as well. Even then I was convinced it was a fluke!

Simon and I planted a church in Crewe during our time at Bible College, and we had a meeting to help the people who attended our church to discover the spiritual and practical gifts God had given them. We were given a sheet of paper and had to fill in the answers. As soon as I was given the questions I felt physically sick. I wanted to cry and run out of the room. Fortunately for me, Amy was only a few months old and provided the perfect escape route. I jumped up and said I thought I could hear the baby crying, so I needed to attend to her. She was fast asleep, but I didn't go back until I was sure the meeting was finished.

After everyone had gone, I told Simon I wasn't going to any more meetings as I felt so thick. The poor man has spent so many hours trying to sort me out over the years! I honestly didn't understand how he could love me as I was. Living in fear of failure affected all areas of my life and made me feel like a rubbish wife, mother, daughter, sister and friend. I felt inferior to everyone, and that I didn't belong anywhere. In my eyes, I was completely useless.

I remember going to morning devotions at college each week and feeling fine when I went into the chapel, but as soon as the worship started I would look at the women leading us and start to feel really down. I envied their gifts and looks and wished I could be just like them. Beryl Glass, whom I didn't really know at Bible college but is now a close friend, used to play the grand piano. I would watch her playing, with beautiful long hair flowing down her back, and want to be her. That was enough to send me into a downward spiral, thinking how unfair it was that all these other ladies were so gifted, clever and beautiful.

Steve Jobs said: "Your time is limited, so don't waste it living someone else's life."[13]

Simon regularly used to quote 1 Corinthians 15:10 to me because God had used it to help him accept who he was and become the person God had created him to be, rather than simply fulfilling the tendency to become someone else or to please people:

> *"But by the grace of God I am what I am, and his grace to me was not without effect…"*

I would shout at him, making it clear that I didn't like who I was. I wanted to be someone else… *anybody* else! I didn't know anyone who was as thick as me.

In her book, *How to Succeed at Being Yourself,* Joyce Meyer writes that one thing she has discovered during her many years in ministry is that most people don't like themselves. This is incredibly sad. I must admit that I spent many years not appreciating who I was. Like Simon, I had to discover that God had created me as I was. I had to learn to accept myself and enjoy being the person God had created me to be.

A rope around my neck

We had a terrible period at the church in Crewe, which we were pastoring, and I allowed the enemy to rob me of a whole year of my life. Some close friends had let us down big time and caused us immense pain and distress. I was totally devastated and nearly had a complete mental breakdown. I wouldn't let anyone get close to me; in fact, I would go to the service but leave before the first song had finished. I felt destroyed by what had happened and almost became housebound. I even struggled to pick Amy up from school.

We were going to the annual Elim Conference at Prestatyn that year, but I really wasn't looking forward to it. Simon said that he felt sure God would speak to me about my future there, but I just laughed at him, thinking, *Yeah, yeah*.

As we walked into the booking hall I saw someone I knew I needed to put things right with. I didn't believe I had done anything wrong, and I had already forgiven the person, but I felt God tell me to be the bigger person and make sure our relationship was restored. It wasn't the easiest thing in the world to do, but I knew I had to be obedient, so that's what I did.

A couple of days later, Regents Theological College launched a new School of Ministry. It was for people who felt called to ministry but were not particularly academic. It involved more practical skills, and I felt God say, "You can do this." In my head I thought, *No way!*, so I didn't bother mentioning it to Simon.

The following day we were getting ready for the evening meeting in our chalet when Simon shouted out from the bathroom,

"I know what you should do. You should do the School of Ministry course."

I laughed and said, "I felt God say that to me the other day, but there's no way I can do it."

He said, "Pray about it and see."

I remember thinking about Abraham's wife Sarah, who laughed when God said she would bear a child despite her advanced years (which she did) and wondering whether it might be possible for me to do the course. Then I pushed it to the back of my mind.

A few days later we were at an evening meeting and a man I had never heard of was preaching. He said, "Some of you sitting here tonight will never achieve your purpose in Christ because you won't do that new course or start that new job because you're so afraid of failing."

I thought, *"Wow! He's talking directly to me!*

At the end of the sermon, he offered ministry time for anyone who wanted prayer. I ran down to the front, as I was desperate for God to set me free.

A minister prayed for me, but I felt nothing. I was so disappointed that I just stayed where I was, having a conversation with God in my mind. Then a pastor from Wales, Paul Houiellebecq, asked if he could pray for me. He started praying and then stopped. He said that he saw me with a rope wrapped around my neck, and that every time I moved forward it pulled me back. He said he didn't know what it meant. I started to cry and said that every time I tried to do something I felt like a failure and stopped because I didn't feel I could do it.

Paul started to pray again, asking God to cut the rope. He physically used his hands as if he were cutting a rope, asking God to set me free from my past and release me into my destiny. I knew that God had set me free once and for all that night. I immediately went to sign up for the School of Ministry course.

The importance of forgiveness

I believe the ministry I received and forgiving that person the day we arrived at Prestatyn were both keys to me being set free from my fear of failure. We can't live in freedom if we're holding unforgiveness in our hearts. The two concepts cannot walk side by side. If you are holding anything against someone, I would urge you to deal with it. You may want to pause now and ask God if there is anyone you need to forgive. If there is, maybe you could pray the following:

"Father, forgive me for not forgiving [insert the person's name here]. I'm sorry for holding a grudge against him/her and I choose today to forgive him/her for what he/she has done to me. Please forgive me for my part in this situation and for holding unforgiveness in my heart. Fill me with your love and peace as I move forward into all that you have for me. Amen."

Forgiving that person should be a turning point, and you should be able to move forward, but in some instances, it may be a bit harder. You may need to keep praying for forgiveness and asking God to help you every time you think about the person. If you're really struggling to forgive someone, you may need to seek help from your church leaders or a Christian friend you can trust.

Being set free didn't mean that I never struggled again. I did, but I had to learn to walk in my new-found freedom and forgiveness. There were days when I had moments of doubt that God had set me free from failure, but as time went on I became more confident that God had really set me free.

Many times as I was writing this book I heard a voice inside me say, *Who do you think you are, writing a book? You couldn't even write an essay properly, let alone a book!* Each time I heard that voice I stopped and reminded myself of that night when I was set free, and all that God has achieved in and through me since that moment.

You may believe that you are a failure right now, but if so I would encourage you to do an audit of your life. I'm sure that when you look back you will discover that you have run your home well or that you are a great parent or a faithful friend, or that you have achieved amazing things at school, work or church. It may well be that while the enemy of your soul is constantly whispering "Failure! Failure!" in your ear, you are really succeeding in the season of life you have found yourself in. You may also discover that others are looking at your life and looking up to you.

Failing doesn't make you a failure

I love Kentucky Fried Chicken. However, did you know that Colonel Sanders, who created the original recipe, failed many times before he became a successful restaurateur? He left school at thirteen to seek his fortune and was unsuccessful working on the railroads and in the army. He was rejected from law school and somehow failed in the insurance industry as well.

At the age of sixty-five he found himself penniless and decided to sell his favourite chicken recipe to restaurant owners. He claims that he was rejected 1,009 times before someone finally said yes to his recipe. This was the beginning of KFC as we know it today. Colonel Sanders is said to have sold the business to investors in 1964 for $2 million. I'm sure he would admit that he had failed big time throughout his life, but he believed that: "Every failure can be a stepping stone to something better."[14]

I want to encourage you that failing doesn't make you a failure. We all make mistakes and struggle to succeed in some areas of our lives. The important thing is that – with God's help – we get up, dust ourselves down and start again.

Over the years there have been many people like Colonel Sanders who have refused to give up when they have apparently failed. Consider Abraham Lincoln, Elvis Presley, Sir James Dyson, Henry Ford, Elizabeth Arden, Bill Gates, Oprah Winfrey, Mary Kay and Steven Spielberg, to name but a few. Just think of all the things those people would have missed out on if they had given up, not to mention what the world would have gone without.

"For we are God's handiwork, created in Christ Jesus to do good works, which God prepared in advance for us to do" (Ephesians 2:10).

God has given each of us a rich destiny however getting there will always cost us something. If we want to achieve anything in life we will have to work at it. We can't just rest on our laurels and hope that everything will fall into place.

Failure can actually make us more determined if we stay focused on the future and on our potential. Our past difficulties and failures must be allowed to shape rather than define us. They will help to make us into the people God wants us to be.

Satan does not want us to move forward into the life God has for us and will do everything in his power to stop us in our tracks. He wants us to remain stuck where we are and will constantly remind us of our past disappointments. We cannot allow that to happen if we want to live the best lives God has for us. If you're struggling in this area, ask your pastor, church leader or a Christian friend to pray with you.

I wish now that I hadn't allowed failure to steal so much of my life. God has used my past for good so much since he set me free, but I have undoubtedly missed out on things I know I could have done but was afraid to do. I am now determined to take hold of every opportunity he gives me. I have told him that if he asks me to do something and I'm available to do it I will always take that step of faith. I can't keep praying, "God, use me", then every time someone asks me to speak at an event or I feel led to start a new ministry I refuse to do it. That's not being obedient to the God I serve.

Whenever God asks us to take on a fresh challenge or do something for the first time, we will often have doubts, fears and anxieties about stepping out into the unknown. However, I've decided to put them to one side because I know that God is with me and will help me. He will never ask us to do anything we are incapable of doing with his help. The God I serve isn't like that. He only wants the best for me.

Perhaps it's time for you to step out of that place of failure and into the destiny God created you for before the beginning of time. Isn't that an exciting thought? But first, how about praying this prayer?

"Father, I bring my feelings of failure before you today. Please help me let go of it once and for all. Forgive me for allowing these feelings to take hold of my life and to stop me doing all the things you have planned for me. Help me to stop comparing myself to others, to focus on you and to start walking in the freedom you have given me. I declare that I am your child, much-loved and created uniquely for your purposes. I refuse to see myself as a failure any longer. I choose to see myself as you see me: forgiven, equipped, gifted, able and empowered by the Holy Spirit for works prepared in advance for me to do. In Jesus' name. Amen."

Chapter 11

Walking in Freedom

"For we are God's masterpiece. He has created us anew in Christ Jesus, so we can do the good things he planned for us long ago."
(Ephesians 2:10, NLT)

I started at the School of Ministry in fear and trepidation back in early September 2001. I was so nervous that first day. I had got up early to do all the things I needed to do before I left the house. I was so fearful of being late, as the thought of walking in after everyone else terrified me.

During my induction, I had asked the course leaders if they would mind not telling the rest of the students I was a pastor's wife because I wanted people to accept me as I was. Sometimes people have false expectations of a pastor's wife, often thinking we can do everything from leading the ladies' prayer meeting and Bible study to counselling, flower arranging, baking, playing the keyboard and leading the worship. I wanted to go under the radar and just enjoy the course. I think people sometimes forget that pastors and their spouses are normal humans. We all have our issues and we aren't all as multitalented as some may think!

The first meeting was simply a chance to get to know everyone. I was immediately introduced to the class as the wife of

Simon Lawton, pastor at New Life Community Church in Crewe. My heart sank! It was set to be a hard enough day as it was, and I really had to cling to the fact that I had been released from my fear of failure and walk in my new-found freedom.

The next day we started lectures. Again, I was nervous, but I knew that with God's help I could get through it. Five minutes into the lecture, a wasp stung me on my neck. I wafted it away, and although it really hurt I tried not to let it affect me. I didn't want to make a scene, as I was struggling enough with my emotions as it was.

The pesky wasp must then have climbed up the other side of my neck and stung me on the face. I jumped up and let out a scream. Fighting back my tears, I explained what had happened. The lecturer said, "Let us pray for our dear sister."

I thought in my head, *I don't need your prayers. I just need to get out of here!* I left the classroom before they could pray for me and headed to the admin office, where a friend of mine worked. She fetched the first-aid kit and tried to calm me down, reassuring me that everything was OK, as I had already made up my mind to go home. I knew in my heart that I had to go back to the classroom and finish the day.

Once our lectures were finished I went home and headed straight up to the bedroom. Simon followed me up and asked how the day had gone. I told him it had been awful and that I was never, ever going back. What a nightmare start! Everything that could have gone wrong did.

Sticking with it

I did return the following day, and the next, and I eventually completed the course. There were many difficult moments and countless times when I felt I couldn't do it, but I clung to the fact that God had set me free from failure. He never said that following him would be easy, but I knew that with God on my side I could do it.

As I look back now, I realise that he also healed and made me whole during that time, and by the end I felt ready to get involved in church life again. I can also see that the enemy sensed my unfulfilled potential and really didn't want me to be set free from my constant feeling of failure. If he could keep me thinking that I wasn't able to do anything it would stop me sharing my faith, using my gifts and making a difference for Jesus.

One of my favourite verses, which I regularly speak over my life, especially when I'm about to step out of my comfort zone, is Philippians 4:13:

"I can do all things through Christ who strengthens me" (NKJV).

Yes, I can do *all* things through Jesus! This verse has changed my thinking. We can be so tied up in knots by our failings, and by the things we haven't achieved, forgetting that if we read God's Word and believe it, we can transform not only our world but other people's worlds as well. The fact that someone has failed at something doesn't make them a failure. It is what we do after we have failed that counts. We can learn so much from our failings and become more successful as a result of them.

Before I was set free, I automatically would have thought, *I can't do this*, whenever a new opportunity to serve God arose, but since that night I have been able to remind myself that he set me free from failure, and that with him by my side I *can* do it. Satan still reminds me of my failures on occasion, but now when this happens I remind myself of all the things I have done since I was set free.

When you truly begin to walk in freedom, God will create opportunities and open doors for you to walk through. That way, you won't simply experience your new-found freedom in your heart; you will live it out in your everyday life. You will also begin to fulfil the plans and purposes he created you for.

Stepping Out

I was helping out at the church's mums and tots group when the two ladies who had been running it decided to step down. As we didn't have anyone else to take it on, Simon said that if I didn't do so we would have to close it. No pressure there, then!

It was one of the best toddler groups around at the time, and all the health visitors in the area recommended it. I really didn't want to lead it, as I felt I had served my time working with children. I often used to say that I didn't like children, and people would say, "But you have five!" This was a valid point, and I loved them all dearly, but I didn't want to look after anyone else's! I had run Sunday school for years and wanted a break from kids. I had only really helped out at the toddler group because I loved drawing alongside the mums and getting to know them.

After much prayer and consideration, I decided to lead it. There was a good team in place to support me, and I felt that if this meant we could keep it open it was worth giving it a go, although I wasn't keen on doing the singing part.

When I met with the ladies who were stepping down, they said, "Don't forget that the song and dance group on the Friday needs leading as well." I replied that there was absolutely no way I could do that, and as it was only a small group it would have to close. But after praying and thinking about it, I agreed to go along and see what it was like.

It turned out that I really enjoyed it, but as I stood in the circle, singing and dancing, I knew I couldn't possibly have led anything like that. However, I ended up sharing my testimony with three ladies at the end of the class. That was where I felt most comfortable, and it was easy, as the ladies were lovely. Nevertheless, I went home ready to tell Simon that I wouldn't be taking it on, and it would have to close.

As I drove home, I felt God say to me, "On one hand you say you love these ladies and want to share your faith with them, but on the other hand you're not prepared to run the group they love so much." Goodness, that really hit me! *Am I going to walk in my new-found freedom or allow my past to come back and wreck my future?* I asked myself. I wasn't prepared to let that happen this time, so I decided to take the new role on.

I attended for the rest of the term to learn the songs and dance moves. I loved it, but I still really wasn't sure how I was going to lead this amazing group.

I spent the hour before my first week in charge in the ladies' toilets. I was so nervous that I was physically sick. I prayed with the team before we got going, then we started the session and really went for it. I couldn't believe how well it went!

The group grew and grew, and it ended up becoming my favourite ministry at the Crewe church. Apart from our children, this group was the thing I missed most when God moved us on to pastor a church in Newcastle.

When we are obedient to God and step outside our comfort zones, God steps in and helps us. We can achieve more than we could ever imagine if we just trust in him.

God wants us to be free and remain free

The fact is, God wants us to be free. Free to become everything he created us to be. Free to be ourselves; comfortable in our own skins and using the personalities, gifts, abilities, talents and experiences that have moulded us into the people we are.

Jesus made many powerful statements, two of which are particularly relevant here:

"So if the Son sets you free, you will be free indeed" (John 8:36).

"The thief comes only to steal and kill and destroy; I have come that they may have life, and have it to the full" (John 10:10).

Jesus came to give us life. Not a life that keeps us bound by fear, failure or anything else, but a life in all its fullness. He wants us to live in freedom so we can fulfil our destiny.

The thief, Satan, wants to rob us of that. He wants to destroy us. If he can keep us believing his lies, he will have achieved what he set out to do. He will often attack us after we have been set free from something (for me it was failure) and have decided to take God at his word and step into all that he has called us to do.

As soon as we begin to serve God or take up a new position, all hell often breaks loose! As I found at the start of my ministry course, everything that could go wrong does. We may experience lack, challenges, attacks, ill health or unexpected opposition, but we should take these things as a good sign! The enemy is determined not just to stop us in our tracks but to thwart God's plans and purposes. We must keep going and enjoy walking in our newfound freedom.

I have experienced many heartaches and hurts in my life: Nigel dying, best friends letting me down and people coming close to disowning me when I married Simon. I could sit and think about this all day and I would be constantly living in a pit. Instead, I recognise that I only have one life; this is not a dress rehearsal. It's important to realise that we only get one chance at it, so let's make the most of the journey, even when opposition comes along.

With God on our side we can live the best lives he has for us. When God set me free, I made a promise to myself that I would never allow Satan to rob me of my freedom again. These days: "When the going gets tough, Julia stands her ground!" It isn't always easy, but I remind myself what I have been set free from and that I never want to go back there again.

Don't look back

Walking in freedom is a choice. We have to be determined and disciplined if we want to live without constraint. If we keep one eye on the past, it will drag us back down. We need to keep moving forward with anticipation, expecting God to use us in new and exciting ways.

> *"Forget the former things; do not dwell on the past. See, I am doing a new thing! Now it springs up; do you not perceive it? I am making a way in the wilderness and streams in the wasteland"* (Isaiah 43:18-19).

I wrote this chapter at our dining room table with a window before and behind me. As I was looked out of the window in front of me, I saw blue sky and lovely autumnal colours in the garden. Suddenly, I saw a reflection on my screen from the window behind me of what I thought was a white van pulling up onto our drive. When I looked around it wasn't a white van but a red one.

I felt God remind me that if we focus on what is ahead we will see all the good things he has for us and our past failures will become a distant memory. But if we keep looking at reflections of the past we won't see things as they really are. We can't turn the clock back and change the past, but we can change the future by moving forward without any regrets and living our lives the best way we can.

Bad things sometimes happen to good people, and in my experience most people have been through at least one major difficulty. We are not exempt from this because we know Jesus, and life can be very tough at times. But with God's help we can navigate through these trials and come out the other side stronger, more determined and more fruitful. And when we do so, we will feel more fulfilled than ever before.

As the saying goes: "If God has saved you out of a sewer, don't dive back in and swim around."

If you're struggling, I would encourage you not to look back but to keep moving forward. Who knows the plans and purposes God has for you? Don't miss out on them by looking back!

Accept who you are

God created you, loves you and accepts you as you are. You are completely unique. Perhaps it's time to accept yourself as well. Learn to be content with the person God created you to be; with the mixture of strengths and weaknesses, gifts and abilities. Then learn to *enjoy* being that person. The world needs you to be you!

At the height of the Covid-19 pandemic we all became used to wearing face masks. Even though they only partially covered our faces, people couldn't really tell what we were thinking or whether we were feeling happy, sad, frustrated or disappointed.

The bigger the face mask, the less people see of our faces and the more our vision is obscured.

I used to live behind an invisible mask of my own making. If someone asked me how I was, I always replied, "Fine, thanks." We have all worn masks like this on occasion so people can't see who we really are. I spent many years hiding my real life from people, only letting them see what I thought they wanted to see. Taking our masks off will allow others to see us for who we are; the incredible people God made in his own image.

> *"For you created my inmost being; you knit me together in my mother's womb. I praise you because I am fearfully and wonderfully made; your works are wonderful, I know that full well. My frame was not hidden from you when I was made in the secret place, when I was woven together in the depths of the earth. Your eyes saw my unformed body; all the days ordained for me were written in your book before one of them came to be"* (Psalm 139:13-16).

American pastor Craig Groeschel wrote: "You are not who others say you are. You are who Christ says you are."[15]

And he's right. We aren't who others say we are; we are who *God* says we are. We are not mistakes. We were created in his image. We are beautiful. As the psalm above says, we are fearfully and wonderfully made. God took great delight in creating us.

In *Straight Talk*, Joyce Meyer writes: "God approved of us before anybody else ever got a chance to disapprove."[16] It doesn't matter what others think of us. We need to look to him, not people. We need to embody God's thoughts about us.

Taking our masks off allows others to see us as we truly are. I've tried to write this book with my mask fully off. It's been a challenge for me to be so transparent, but I hope it will help you to be brave and allow people to see you as you truly are with your flaws, weaknesses, insecurities, anxieties and fears. It might help the people closest to you to know and understand the battles you're currently fighting. You may well discover that you're not on your own; that others are fighting similar battles.

Let God use your experience to benefit others

God often uses our past experiences to minister to others. Rick Warren once said that: "Your worst days can lead to your best opportunities for growth and ministry. God never wastes a hurt. He doesn't want you to just trudge through it. He wants you to mature through it, and then use your experience to help others facing the same situation."[17]

The apostle Paul wrote something similar:

> "He comforts us in all our troubles so that we can comfort others. When they are troubled, we will be able to give them the same comfort God has given us" (2 Corinthians 1:4, NLT).

It can make us vulnerable when we take the mask off and start walking in freedom, but that just shows people who we really are... warts and all! We may get hurt again in the future, but if God is for us who can be against us, as Romans 8:1 says? He has our backs. He is in charge. Going through challenges, difficulties and dark days will make us better people and help us become the people God really wants us to be.

I have found that it's much better to be myself than to hide behind a mask. It's such hard work trying to be people we are not and can make us feel quite exhausted. Being ourselves is much more fun and a lot less stressful.

Taking my mask off gave me the confidence to be myself, follow my passions and immerse myself in the things that really mattered to me. I began to take more risks, grow in confidence and step into things I never believed I could do.

I had always had a heart for the community and felt there were ways we could help people less fortunate than ourselves. I was aware that I had been incredibly blessed, as I could have been in a terrible position financially after Nigel died. Had I not had such wonderful family on both sides supporting me, I hate to think where I would have ended up.

In light of this, I decided to get involved with the local women's refuge in Crewe, buying essential items the women would need when they entered the refuge. I would say to the ladies at church, "Imagine if you had to leave your home in the middle of the night with your children, and all you had were the clothes you were standing up in." Then I encouraged them to place one item in their shopping trolley each week so we could help keep the emergency cupboard at the refuge well stocked.

We made hampers at Christmas and provided presents for the children. We took them to the refuge and to many women who had been rehoused in the community. We also took chocolate eggs at Easter, school backpacks filled with stationary in September and anything else we thought might be useful throughout the year. In addition, we sponsored some of the children to attend the kids' camp we ran in Wales.

If you had asked me a year earlier if I could have taken this work on I would have laughed, but by this point I knew that anything was possible with God. It was such a blessing to be used by him in this way, and to see people's lives change as a result.

New opportunities in Newcastle

I was so fortunate that God enabled me to start walking in freedom before he called us to Elim Church Newcastle in August 2008. He had prepared me well for this next season, where I was given the freedom to move forward into other fantastic new opportunities. Yet again, his timing was perfect, as I wouldn't have been able to done any of it if God hadn't been at work in my life beforehand.

I really began to flourish in Newcastle. Yes, this woman who had lived in a place of failure most of her life, and whose confidence had been further knocked by the loss of her husband, finally started to come into her own. I'm not saying any of this to glorify myself, but to demonstrate that there is life after loss, and that God will open doors and create opportunities tailored to your unique gifts, abilities, experiences and passions if you allow him to do so.

Simon and I were driving to the church in the middle of winter the first year we were in Newcastle when we noticed that many of the children weren't wearing coats. If you've ever been to the North East in winter, you'll know that it can be absolutely freezing with the cold winds blowing in off the North Sea. The following day I saw a Save the Children statistic which estimated that 1.6 million UK children were living in poverty and parents couldn't afford to feed their children properly.[18] I realised that if they couldn't feed their kids, they certainly wouldn't have enough money to buy them clothes.

I decided right then that we had to do something about it, so we launched Coats4Kids. I asked everyone at the church if they would be willing to either buy a coat or donate money to buy one for a primary school child. The church family was amazing and we gave away more than forty brand-new coats the first year. We built strong links with local schools, and over the years this number grew to more than one hundred. We never had to buy any of the coats with church funds because God provided through the congregation and the wider community. People loved buying coats for us and the children were grateful recipients.

What started as a seemingly random thought on the way to church one day became a successful ministry, and I later helped launch it at several other Elim churches. God planted a seed and it grew! I want to challenge you today. If you have a small (or big!) idea that God has placed in your heart, run with it. You never know what you will achieve until you have a go. In the natural you might fail, but if it's a God idea you will succeed. You may even end up with a nationwide ministry or business on your hands.

Over time, I launched other ministries in Newcastle:

Clothes store

Simon had visited the Dream Centre in Los Angeles and come back with a passion to open a clothes store. My heart was for the community around us, so I was really excited about this. We opened the store one day a week and it became an instant success. Clients came from all over Newcastle to receive free clothes and they all loved it. We tried to give them a personal shopping experience, with our volunteers taking them around and helping them select appropriate items.

I remember wondering before it opened how on earth were we going to replenish the stock each week. Our church members had been fantastic with their initial donations, but they wouldn't be able to bring additional items every week. Fortunately, the local paper printed a story about what we were doing, and before long we were inundated with clothes, toys and anything else people wanted to get rid of. We never had to ask for any donations; the clothes just kept coming.

It was overwhelming at first, but incredible to see how God had brought everything together. We saw salvations and healings as clients sat and enjoyed free home-made soup, cakes and other refreshments. Other churches across the nation liked the idea and opened their own clothes banks. We were able to show them around and tell them what had worked best for us.

1st Babeeze

We also decided to help the young mums in our area by making up baby changing bags for them that contained everything they would need for their new babies, plus a bag for mum containing practical items and some treats for her stay in hospital. The mid-wives in Newcastle and at health centres near the church used to refer mums to us.

Seeing the mums' faces when they started looking through their bags was so rewarding. Most of them couldn't believe that anyone would give them something for nothing. We were then able to signpost them to the clothes store and get to know some of them better. Often we would be able to give them prams, cots, Moses baskets and other items that had been donated to us as well.

2nd Steps

Six weeks later we would invite the mums back and bless them with a 2nd Steps bag filled with more baby items, plus a weaning bag containing everything they would need for the next stage in their babies' lives.

Adopt a Block

Adopt a Block was a ministry where we went out to sweep the paths and collect litter in the community around the church. We knocked on residents' doors and offered to do jobs for them, such as rubbish removal, painting, gardening or home visits if they were lonely. Anything we could physically do for them, we did. We also took people Easter and Christmas gifts to let them know how much we cared.

Aspire

One of the ministries I launched was Aspire Newcastle, linked to Elim's national Aspire women's ministry, which raised money for Elim Missions every time we met. God allowed me to minister to the ladies myself and bring other speakers in. We had socials, prayer and worship meetings, pamper sessions, and craft and testimony nights. I helped prepare some of our ladies to preach for their first time, and from there they went on to preach in the main church and speak at ladies' conferences. It was such an exciting and fulfilling time in my life.

One of my happiest memories is of a time when I invited my friend Lesley Beattie, whose husband was a pastor in Sunderland, to come and minister to the ladies. She asked if she could bring her sister Helen Sabais along, who had grown up in a pastor's home but wasn't going on with God. Lesley said that she doubted that Helen would come, as she had invited her to many things in the past. Helen often said yes but then never came.

Helen did come on this occasion, and from the moment she arrived she felt God's presence. In fact, she cried all the way through the worship, and by the end of the evening she had recommitted her life to Jesus. From that day forward she attended the church and rarely missed a service.

Helen's life was transformed, and she ended up bringing her husband Martin to church. He was later saved and baptised, and before long Helen and Martin became key people in the life of the church. They got involved with the food bank and were such a blessing to people in and outside the church. By the time Simon and I left the church, Helen was the food bank administrator and Martin was managing the church's gift aid account and handling the clothes store's admin.

Lesley could have stopped asking her sister to events because Helen never turned up. But Jesus never gives up on us, so we should never give up on people, as hard as that may seem some days. I am so grateful to Lesley for persevering, as I would never have had the privilege of calling this fabulous couple true friends if she had.

Aspire went from strength to strength, and out of it we birthed our Faith, Hope and Love Conference. This was one of the highlights of the year for many ladies in the North East. My heart was to bless the ladies in every way we could think of. We wanted them to feel loved from the minute they walked into the Dream Centre.

We gave away free conference tickets to the ladies who came to our food bank and clothes store, as we didn't just want the day to be about women from the church, but also about reaching into the community. After the first conference, one lady said she felt as if she had been to a spa day, and that she had left feeling extremely relaxed and spoiled. Many ladies gave their lives to Jesus at this conference over the years.

What others saw

One of the many things I have learned is that other people will often see potential in us even when we don't. So if they ask you to do something, it's not because they feel sorry for you! It's because they see hidden promise in you and want to release you into it.

My friend Julia Derbyshire asked me to speak to the women at City Gates Church in Ilford (where I recently heard Amy speak), which she runs with her husband Stephen. She asked me to share my testimony and preach about failure. I agreed, but I kept asking myself why she would ask me, as I felt so out of my depth. To my amazement, what I shared was really well received, and I was able to pray with several ladies who were struggling with grief and failure.

A few months later I was chatting to Julia and said that I couldn't work out why she had asked me to speak. She had never even heard me share my testimony. Julia replied that she had seen something in me and simply knew that I had a powerful story to tell.

I was even more surprised when Marilyn Glass, leader of Elim's national ladies' ministry Aspire asked me to join her team as regional leader for the North East. I had seen some of the amazing, multitalented women on the team interviewed in *Direction* magazine and felt physically sick wondering how and where I would fit in. I was convinced that if I joined the team I would get found out; that they would see I was not the person they thought I was. I really don't know what I thought that was, as most of them didn't even know me! Simon encouraged me, pointing out that Marilyn wouldn't have asked me if she didn't think I could do it. So I accepted her offer.

As we sat around the boardroom table at the first meeting, my fears and failures began to overwhelm me. *What on earth am I doing here?* I asked myself. I was so out of my depth I felt as though I was drowning. The ladies were all fantastic, however, and over time I realised I was on the team because I had something to bring. We all have different gifts, personalities and experiences, and we all have a part to play.

> *"So in Christ we, though many, form one body, and each member belongs to all the others. We have different gifts, according to the grace given to each of us..."* (Romans 12:5-6).

Even now when we have team meetings, I look around the table and listen to everyone's amazing ideas and those old feelings of failure try to settle on me. I begin to feel inadequate and have to tell myself that God has set me free; that he placed me on this team for a reason. I have to focus on what is true and refute the enemy's lies. It is important that:

> *"...we take captive every thought to make it obedient to Christ"* (2 Corinthians 10:5).

In one of her motivational videos, speaker and author Jen Baker said: "Wherever the enemy lies, we know that is where our purpose lies."[19]

I have discovered over time that Jesus will set us free, but we have to walk in and fight for this freedom. The devil plays dirty, so we have to choose to remain free and not get drawn back into a place of containment and control.

I will always be thankful to Marilyn for giving me that opportunity and for seeing the potential in me. Being on the team has helped me grow in Christ in numerous ways and has pushed me out into deeper waters at times when I would naturally have shrunk back. I have also made lifelong friends with women who support, encourage and cheer me on, and are there when I need them. I'm so glad I have each and every one of them in my life. With God's help, they have made me a much better person.

Grasp the opportunities God gives you

Another thing I have learned from my journey is that we need to grasp every opportunity God gives us. We never know what these new ventures might bring. Simon and I have been to places and done things I could only have dreamed of back in the day. I never imagined that my life could be so exciting and fulfilling! If you are living in a place of failure, please allow God to set you free today so you can move forward into all the incredible things he has for you. With God by your side, you can do *all* things.

Who would have thought when I sat in Nigel's favourite chair that evening in 1986, devastated and broken, holding his sweatshirt against my face and believing my life was over, that God would turn things around to the extent he has? He is the restorer and rebuilder of broken lives. I have seen it in my own life and in many other people's lives, and I believe you will see it in yours.

I love the way *The Message* version translates Jeremiah's words:

> *"I'll never forget the trouble, the utter lostness, the taste of ashes, the poison I've swallowed. I remember it all – oh, how well I remember – the feeling of hitting the bottom. But there's one other thing I remember, and remembering, I keep a grip on hope: God's loyal love couldn't have run out, his merciful love couldn't have dried up. They're created new every morning. How great your faithfulness! I'm sticking with God (I say it over and over). He's all I've got left"* (Lamentations 3:19-24).

Chapter 12

The end of the beginning

"This is not the end. It is not even the beginning of the end.
But it is, perhaps, the end of the beginning"
(Sir Winston Churchill)[20]

I truly believed my life was over when I lost Nigel. It felt as if I had lost everything. I lost all hope and couldn't see any future at all. Yes, I had my boys, whom I loved dearly, but I felt lonely, isolated and fearful. How could I face the next day and the day after that without Nigel? Life as I knew it was over. It really felt like the end.

If you have lost someone close, particularly a spouse, close family member or friend, my heart goes out to you, but I want to say to you, softly and gently, that your life is not over. Although you didn't ask for it to happen, a page has been turned and a new chapter has commenced.

As Winston Churchill suggested in the quote above, what appears to be the end is often the end of the beginning. That is perhaps a helpful way of viewing it. You are not alone. God is still with you, and he certainly hasn't forgotten you.

"Father of the fatherless and protector of widows is God in his holy habitation" (Psalm 68:5, ESV).

This verse applies to anyone who has lost someone close. Sometimes it takes a while for God's plans to be revealed, so you may need to be patient while God is at work. But he is there for you, and he has a plan. A *good* plan.

He heals the brokenhearted

The Bible says: *"He heals the brokenhearted and binds up their wounds"* (Psalm 147:3). God is close to the broken-hearted and hears your cry, so cry out to him. Lean on him and allow him to start or continue the process of healing.

Jesus healed my broken heart, but it didn't happen overnight. It occurred over a period of time. That doesn't mean I never shed a few tears or feel sad these days, for instance when I visit Nigel's grave or when I look at the boys when they are doing something that Nigel might have done. It simply means that my life isn't one of constant pain and living in the past any more. God has loved and comforted me throughout the journey I have been on, and he can do the same for you.

God is the source of all comfort. He often comforts me through his Word as I read my daily devotional. I have often found that the verse or passage I'm reading is so appropriate for how I'm feeling at the time, which encourages me and reminds me he is with me. Sometimes when I'm struggling, I actively look for a scripture that will help me, then I read it again and again, allowing it to sink deep into my spirit.

Most of us live in countries where the Bible is readily available, so I would encourage you to visit it regularly. You'll be amazed how often the words you are reading are appropriate and timely for the particular moment you are in or the situation you are facing. We shouldn't be surprised by this, as the Word of God is alive and active (see Hebrews 4:12), and I believe that God actively reaches into our lives and circumstances with it.

God has also used other people to comfort me on many occasions. It could be a card through the post, a phone call, a gift or someone spending time with me. I also remember going to several conferences and Sunday services when I didn't feel like being there, and it was as if the preacher had written the sermon just for me. God has used various men and women to bring the right word to me at just the right time.

At other times, the tears have flowed down my cheeks as people have prayed with me and the Holy Spirit has ministered to me intimately, working gently to heal my breaking heart. And as you start to heal, you will find that you are able to comfort others who are not as far down the path as you, and that will help you as much as it helps them.

Why don't you stop right now and ask God to comfort you and give you strength when you are feeling weak? Ask him to send his Holy Spirit to minister to you.

He restores

God is our great redeemer and restorer. Not only does he want to take us in all our brokenness and put us back together, but he has wonderful plans to prosper us and not to harm us; to give us a hope and a future. It is my belief that God has much more in store for you than you can imagine right now. Trust him and let him lead.

One of the most frequently quoted Bible verses is this one:

"I will restore to you the years which the swarming locust has eaten..." (Joel 2:25, RSV).

I am living proof that he is a God of restoration. Yes, your life may be different after a bereavement, but I believe that it can still be good. Simon isn't Nigel and Nigel wasn't Simon, but our life is good!

No matter what stage you are at in your grief and loss, no matter what situation you find yourself in, let me encourage you to trust the God of miracles. Be patient and allow him to restore you. God has so much more in store for you. In fact, no matter what age you are, there will still be plans and purposes that God wants you to fulfil.

As Joyce Meyer said: "No matter what we have lost, God can help us recover!"[21]

As I discovered, God had provision, plans, purposes, relationships and adventures for me that I had no idea about. Of course, I have the benefit of hindsight as I write these things, while you may well be at the beginning of your journey. But as I mentioned at the start of this book, I genuinely felt my life was over when Nigel died. Never could I have imagined that God had a plan and a purpose for me, yet here I am more than thirty years later with a fantastic husband, five children and six grandchildren. My life has been really full, and God is still taking us on all kinds of adventures.

When I consider what I might have missed out on had I given up that first night, I am amazed by his grace and mercy. I'm not saying it was easy – there were many times when I had to hang on for dear life – but I am saying it is worth it. We are all different and are facing different circumstances, and God also works differently in each one of us, at a pace we can handle. It takes longer for some than for others, but you will come through it in the end.

He rebuilds broken lives

If we look at the story of Ruth and Naomi in the Old Testament, we can see how God is able to put lives back together. Naomi, Elimelek and their two sons, Mahlon and Kilion, left Bethlehem during a time of famine to live in the country of Moab. While they were there, Elimelek died, leaving Naomi with her two sons, who married Moabite women, Orpah and Ruth. About ten years later, Mahlon and Kilion died.

Naomi was absolutely distraught after her husband and both sons died. She must have felt as though she had lost everything. She decided to return to her home in Bethlehem and urged her daughters-in-law to return to their families. She felt the Lord had turned against her and that it would be better for them if they left her.

They all wept and Orpah returned to her home, but Ruth clung to her mother-in-law and refused to leave. Ruth could have given up and returned to her home, but instead she followed her heart and did what she felt was the honourable thing to do by staying with Naomi. She promised to go wherever Naomi went, declaring that Naomi's people would become her people and that Naomi's God would become her God.

They returned to Bethlehem together in deep anguish and grief:

"...When they arrived in Bethlehem, the whole town was stirred because of them, and the women exclaimed, 'Can this be Naomi?' 'Don't call me Naomi,' she told them. 'Call me Mara, because the Almighty has made my life very bitter. I went away full, but the Lord has brought me back empty.

Why call me Naomi? The Lord has afflicted me; the Almighty has brought misfortune upon me'" (Ruth 1:19-21).

I guess she must have felt angry with God and completely lost. This is a natural reaction, but although terrible things do happen, we must be careful not to blame God. We live in a sin-filled and sin-impacted world. It's not how God planned it to be, and that is why sometimes bad things happen.

We discover from the Bible narrative that Ruth's love and loyalty to Naomi cost her dearly at first, but she remained at Naomi's side through everything. Ruth was faithful to Naomi and worked in the fields so they had food to eat. She soon found favour with Boaz, a relative of Naomi's husband, who had heard about the way she was caring for her mother-in-law. Boaz eventually proposed to Ruth and they were married. Ruth was blessed with a son whose descendants included King David and Jesus!

What an incredible story of hope and restoration. Ruth was rewarded for her faithfulness. Her life was redeemed and Naomi's life was restored. I am sure it wasn't easy for either woman, but they both knew God was with them. Sometimes that is all we can hang on to. God not only restored and rebuilt their lives; he also achieved his plans and purposes through them. He can do the same for each one of us. He can do it for you.

He sustains

No matter your age, situation or loss, God's promise is this:

"Even to your old age and grey hairs I am he, I am he who will sustain you. I have made you and I will carry you; I will sustain you and I will rescue you" (Isaiah 46:4).

I have certainly found this to be true every step of the way. He has always been there for me, and I have been able to lean on him whenever I needed to. He has provided everything I have ever needed physically, practically, emotionally and spiritually.

There were many occasions while Simon was at Bible college that we had eaten our last meal and spent all our money. At times like this we would sit around the table and pray for God's provision as a family. Often the doorbell would ring and we would find an envelope waiting there with money in it, or a letter with a cheque in would arrive.

I remember our washing machine dying and not having the money to replace it. We were a family of seven, one of whom was a newborn, so there was a lot of washing to do! We couldn't afford to keep going to the launderette either, so we prayed and prayed. I don't remember telling anyone about it, but a few days later a brand-new one was delivered to our flat. I have no idea who paid for it, as the only information we had related to the store it had been ordered from, and we didn't know anyone from that area.

I have also seen God heal my children of various things, including Matthew's heart murmur. My friends and home group prayed for God to heal him, and when he went for his next appointment there wasn't a trace of it. On another occasion I was due to have an operation for a ganglion cyst to be removed from my finger. I was prayed for and it disappeared, never to be seen again. God provides, sustains and heals.

I could tell countless stories of how he turned desperate situations to good. I always took our requests to him and he looked after them. They weren't always answered straight away, but I never doubted that he would keep that promise above from Isaiah. And as I look back, I don't think I would have such a strong faith now if God had answered all my prayers instantly.

Let me encourage you to look to him for everything you need. Go to him and tell him what you need each day. He will listen, he will hear your cry and he will answer.

You are stronger than you think (with God's help)

It can be a challenge to get up each morning when you are grieving, and you may wonder how you will find the strength to face each new day. The Bible reminds us that God's mercies are new every morning and great is his faithfulness (see Lamentations 3:22-23). His grace is sufficient for us every day (see 2 Corinthians 12:9).

One of the things I have learned is not to attempt to face the day in my own strength. That is unsustainable at a time of grief and loss. Actually, it is unsustainable at any time. God did not leave us as orphans, but gave us his Holy Spirit to be our strength when we feel weak; our guide when we don't know what to do; our peace when we feel anxious; and our calm when we feel fearful.

"Tragedy will pull strengths out of you that you didn't know you had."[22]

I'm still not entirely sure how I got through those early days, but I am so thankful to God for giving me the strength not to give up but to push through. Even though I had three little boys who needed my constant attention, I managed to find moments (often in the bath!) when I could spend time talking to God, asking him to renew my strength and meet the needs of each new day.

Great advice

One piece of advice I received from my counsellor was that I shouldn't do anything I didn't *need* to do if it was too painful. That helped me so much. There are some things we *have* to do, such as feed and clothe our children, but why put ourselves through something we don't feel comfortable or ready to do, or that hurts us, if we don't need to?

For instance, clearing out our loved one's clothes and belongings is always going to be a painful experience. There may come a time when we feel better able to do it. It's worth waiting for that moment.

To all those who are grieving

God chose me to be his daughter and has loved, cared and provided for me every step of the way. He has never let me down and he won't let you down either.

My prayer for anyone who has experienced grief is this: don't bury it and refuse to talk about it. Bring it before God and tell him exactly how you feel.

In the book of Psalms, we discover that David, who himself suffered tragedy, loss, failure and disappointment, poured out his heart to God. I love his honesty in so many of the psalms he wrote. God listens to our anguished cries and ministers to us in the darkest, most painful moments. David encourages us to confide in our Creator:

> *"Trust in him at all times, you people; pour out your hearts to him, for God is our refuge"* (Psalm 62:8).

God is such a good listener and will gently administer his healing balm.

I recognise that men and woman may cope differently with their emotions. Women often like to talk and share with one another, while men tend to bottle things up. For the men reading this, it is not a sign of weakness to share your feelings. If you are struggling, I urge you to find someone who will listen. Please, please don't try to cope alone. You may need to seek professional advice from a doctor or counsellor.

It's also okay to feel sad, angry, disappointed or depressed. You are human and it's normal. Let me encourage you to get the help you need. You will feel so much better if you do, and life won't seem half as difficult.

If you are a widow or a widower, I want you to know that it's okay to fall in love again and have a new beginning. Life is short and our time on earth is precious. When we feel the time is right, we should try to move forward, hard as that may be for our families and friends, and also for ourselves. The people we have lost wouldn't want us to put our lives on hold forever. They would want us to live life in all its fullness. That doesn't mean you have forgotten them; that will never happen! It simply means you have permission to enjoy your life again. As Solomon, in all his wisdom, suggests:

There is a time for everything,
and a season for every activity under the heavens:
a time to be born and a time to die,
a time to plant and a time to uproot,
a time to kill and a time to heal,
a time to tear down and a time to build,
a time to weep and a time to laugh,
a time to mourn and a time to dance,
a time to scatter stones and a time to gather them,

a time to embrace and a time to refrain from embracing,
a time to search and a time to give up,
a time to keep and a time to throw away;
a time to tear and a time to mend,
a time to be silent and a time to speak,
a time to love and a time to hate,
a time for war and a time for peace.
(Ecclesiastes 3:1-8)

Better days lie ahead

The story of Job highlights the personal suffering, tragedy and loss he experienced. He lost everything! The Bible describes him as the greatest man among all the people of the east, and records how he tragically lost seven sons, three daughters and many servants along with his homes and his massive flocks. He was also afflicted with a painful skin complaint that caused sores to form all over his body.

During this terrible ordeal he was encouraged by his friend Bildad, who said:

"[God] will yet fill your mouth with laughter and your lips with shouts of joy" (Job 8:21).

We later read that God fully restored Job:

"...The Lord restored his fortunes and gave him twice as much as he had before... The Lord blessed the latter part of Job's life more than the former part. He had fourteen thousand sheep, six thousand camels, a thousand yoke of oxen and a thousand donkeys. And he also had seven sons and three daughters" (Job 42:10-13).

Meanwhile, David encourages all those who are mourning and grieving with the following:

"Weeping may remain for a night but rejoicing comes in the morning" (Psalm 30:5).

You may feel raw right now, and perhaps you are experiencing incredible pain and anguish. But hold on to the hope that, after a period of grieving, God will begin to restore and rebuild your life. Joy and happiness will be yours once again. Your house will become a place of laughter rather than tears. Things will never be the same, but I believe your future will be good, because God himself is good.

You have to run your own race

One of the many things I have learned on this journey with Jesus is that we need to follow God's advice and not man's. We have to let him lead. If I had listened to a lot of the people around me I would never have married Simon. We wouldn't have gone to Bible college or planted the church in Crewe. We wouldn't have had more children or moved to Newcastle.

We would have missed out on thirty-four years of marriage and two beautiful daughters. Our children might never have met their spouses and had their own beautiful children. There might never have been an incredible church building in Crewe where New Life Community Church was established. And we would have missed all the fun involved in helping God build the Dream Centre and ministering to the local community by clothing, feeding and bringing hope to many people. If we listen to God's voice and follow what he says, we will taste and see that the Lord is good (see Psalm 38:4).

Over the years, Simon and I have followed the call of God into a multitude of new things and many people have commented that we must have been brave to do it. My reply has always been that I actually think it's braver to refuse to go where God has asked us to go. Walking in God's will is the best possible place to be, and that's what I want to do, no matter what it involves. I know he will always look after us when we are in his will.

As a couple, one of our favourite promises is this:

"Trust in the Lord with all your heart and lean not on your own understanding; in all your ways submit to him, and he will make your paths straight" (Proverbs 3:5-6).

We have lived our lives trusting him as far as we possibly can and have seen some incredible things happen. People often let us down; not necessarily deliberately, but because they are human and imperfect, just like us. But Jesus has never let me down. He has never failed to be true to his word. There have been times when I have had to wait a long time for a promise to come to fruition, but I have learned that his timing is perfect. It is never too late or too soon.

Time to surrender to Him

It may be that you need to surrender your plans and ideas of how you think your life should go to God. Why not allow him to take control and lead you into this next season? I know from my own experience that this may mean making sacrifices, but it is always worth it.

"Therefore, I urge you, brothers and sisters, in view of God's mercy, to offer your bodies as a living sacrifice, holy and pleasing

to God – this is your true and proper worship. Do not conform to the pattern of this world, but be transformed by the renewing of your mind. Then you will be able to test and approve what God's will is – his good, pleasing and perfect will" (Romans 12:1-2).

Paul reminds us here that God's plan for us is good, pleasing and perfect. But it always starts with surrender.

As I come to the end of my story, I hope it has helped you understand the journey you are on in some way, and to recognise that the way you have been feeling is normal. It's okay. God knows and understands the pain and loss you are experiencing.

If you are struggling with any of the things I have shared, please seek help. Talk to someone. You don't have to struggle alone.

There is hope in God. The Bible promises that if you delight yourself in the Lord, he will give you the desires and secret petitions of your heart (see Psalm 37:4, AMPC). Let me encourage you to surrender your life to him afresh right now. Trust that your story is not over. It is not the end, but rather the end of the beginning. A page has turned. A new day has dawned, and God is with you in it.

"I know what I'm doing. I have it all planned out – plans to take care of you, not abandon you, plans to give you the future you hope for" (Jeremiah 29:11, MSG).

Do you know God?

The most important decision I ever made was to become a Christian. It changed my life for the better in every way.

If you don't know God personally, I would like to encourage you to find out more about him. There are many ways you can do this. You can attend an Alpha course (www.alpha.org). These introductory courses are hosted by churches in cities and towns around the world.

However, there is nothing to stop you inviting him into your life right now by praying this simple prayer:

"Father God, I bring myself before you today. I don't know everything about you, but I know that I need you in my life. Please forgive me for all the things I've done wrong and wipe the slate of my life clean. I need a new start. I'm choosing to trust you today, and I gladly surrender my life to you. Take me just as I am. Come and live in me by your Holy Spirit. Amen."

If you have prayed this prayer, you have become part of God's worldwide family. This will be the best decision you have ever made.

If you have a friend who is a Christian, tell him or her. I am sure your friend will help you on this new journey. Then find a Bible-believing church. You could email the leaders and tell them what you have done so they can support you.

If you need any help with this or with finding a church nearby, please let me know and I'll try to help.

Further help

There are three organisations offering bereavement support in the UK that I would recommend:

Cruse Bereavement Care: www.cruse.org.uk

This charity was recommended to me after Nigel's death, and I benefited from its services at the time. The organisation provides a much wider-reaching service today, including emotional support for bereaved adults, young people and children. It supports people via email and through a grief chat service, with a trained professional on hand to respond to people's needs.

Loros (www.loros.co.uk, Leicestershire only)

I also received six weeks of counselling from Loros Hospice, which helped enormously, as I needed to talk to people who understood. If you have been bereaved and are struggling, I would strongly encourage you to reach out to Loros or a local equivalent for help. It's not a sign of weakness. We are humans, not robots, and we all need other people. Everyone needs a shoulder to cry on, a listening ear and advice from someone who understands what we are going through at times like this.

Association of Christian Counselling (ACC): www.acc-uk.org

Although I don't have first-hand experience of the ACC, I have heard that its counsellors offer a great service.

Further information

Feedback

I'd love to receive your feedback about this book. Even better, I'd love to see a review on Amazon, Goodreads or wherever you purchased it. Reviews are like gold dust to an author, as they provide insight, credibility and confidence to potential purchasers.

Email

If you have any comments or suggestions, or have noticed any typos, please email me at jealawton@hotmail.co.uk

Connect

Join me on:

Facebook: Julia Lawton
Instagram: julia.lawton.12
Twitter: 1JuliaLawton

IMAGINE

TRUSTING GOD
LIKE NEVER BEFORE

simon lawton

INC. SESSIONS FOR SMALL GROUPS

COURAGE
FOR THE
Discouraged

Steps to restoring faith,
hope and strength

SIMON LAWTON

"This is at heart a book of help and a book of hope."
Chris Cartwright

End notes

1   Queen Elizabeth II, cited by Sapsted, D., Foster, P.
    and Jones G. in "Grief is price of love, says the Queen"
    (*The Telegraph*, 21st September 2001).

2   Rantzen, E., *Living With Grief* (Channel 5, 3rd March
    2021).

3   Kubitz, M., "The Irrationality of Grief" (aliveinmemory.org/
    2014/04/23/the-irrationality-of-grief).

4   Let's Talk About Loss (instagram.com/talkaboutloss, 15th
    May 2021).

5   Stevenson, M., "Footprints in the Sand" (footprints-inthe-
    sand.com).

6   Wilcox, D., *Living With Grief* (Channel Five, 18th
    February 2021).

7   Ward, S., "Like a Wave" (instagram.com/talkaboutloss, 15th
    March 2021).

8   Kübler-Ross, E. and Kessler, D., *On Grief and Grieving:
    Finding the Meaning of Grief Through the Five Stages* (Scribner:
    2005, p. 230).

9   Staff writer, "Understanding the Five Stages of Grief"
    (cruse.org.uk/get-help/five-stages-of-grief).

10 Roth, V., *Insurgent* (HarperCollins Children's Books: 2012,
    p. 377).

11 Duncan, M., *Good Grief* (Lion Hudson: 2020, p. 106).

12 Grylls, B. (twitter.com/beargrylls, 28th August 2015).

13 Jobs, S., cited in "'You've got to find what you love,' Jobs says" (news.stanford.edu/2005/06/14/jobs-061505, 14th June 2005).

14 Sanders, C., "The Biggest Failure in Kentucky" (https://www.kfc.co.uk/colonels-story).

15 Groeschel, C. (twitter.com/craiggroeschel, 5th April 2021).

16 Meyer, J., *Straight Talk on Insecurity: Overcoming Emotional Battles with the Power of God's Word!* (Faith Words: 2003, p. 15).

17 Warren, R., "God Brings Good Out of What Feels Bad" (pastorrick.com/god-brings-good-out-of-what-feels-bad).

18 Jenkins, G., "1.6 Million Children in Severe Poverty Let Down by Budget" (savethechildren.org.uk/blogs/2011/1-6-million-children-in-severe-poverty-let-down-by-budget, 23rd March 2011).

19 Baker, J., "I don't like to give the enemy 'air time' BUT this needs to be said!" (jenbaker.co.uk/vlogs/2021/5/16/i-dont-like-to-give-the-enemy-air-time-but-this-needs-to-be-said, 16th May 2021).

20 Churchill, W., "The End of the Beginning", Winston Churchill: Greatest Speeches (youtube.com/watch?v=1K-rKQYB9ns, 22nd October 2013).

21 Meyer, J. (twitter.com/JoyceMeyer/status/1370743280430907393, 13th March 2021).

22 @graceandgrief (instagram.com/graceandgrief, 7th December 2020).

Printed in Poland
by Amazon Fulfillment
Poland Sp. z o.o., Wrocław

10076802R00094